Foreword

CW00457314

Teaching Science, I have always found myself to be jealous of M
set an exercise from a text book there are always many ques
practice the topic which has just been taught. Not only that but
just from the initial perspective but are rearranged to find a variable which is not the
subject of the equation. After that there are the questions in words rather than numbers
and they always increase in difficulty throughout the exercise.

The most common way in which I try to use text books is to set exercises from them after
the topic has been introduced but I am always disappointed. It is not uncommon to find a
Science text book with just 3 or 4 questions on a topic as wide as, say, momentum and so
we science teachers use worksheets.

Since no book existed that met my needs, I have written one.

The aim of this book is not to show students how to solve Physics problems – the
assumption is that that has already been done by the teacher using any of the methods in
their pedagogical armoury. It is to give the students chance to practice those skills more
than just a couple of times and to attempt problems posed from as many angles as possible.
Where there is an equation, I have set problems which require rearrangement to solve for
all variables. I have given questions in simple numerical form as well as in longer, "wordier"
ways. I have kept pictures to a minimum as I find examinations do this too.

Where appropriate, I have given the formulae in exactly the format of the AQA
Specifications 8463 and 8464. "g" is also given as 9.8 m/s^2 as stated in the specification. I
have noted within the questions whether the formula in question will be given on the
Physics Equation Sheet or whether candidates are expected to recall it. I have varied
units throughout so that students are expected to convert to standard units before using
formulae and, although I have attempted to keep numbers as "tidy" as possible (such as
when students are expected to take a square root), there will be times when they will have
to round to significant figures or decimal places, as stated in Mathematical Requirements
(AQA Specification 8463 page 81 and AQA Specification 8464 page 163).

I have tried to write everything from the point of view of the specification. You will find
specification references at the beginning of every section and I have written questions
relating to everything which appears within the specification. Where a specification
section is small, I have merged it with an appropriate section. A couple of specification
sections (Energy Stored in a Spring and Specific Heat Capacity) are repeated but I have
only put one set of questions for each into the book.

It was only near the end of the writing process that I discovered that the concept of
giving the students lots of examples has a name – SLOP! (Shed Loads Of Practice.) If, like
me, you subscribe to this idea then this book is for you.

This book is written in the Comic Sans Serif font as I had it recommended as the most
readable font by my school's SEN coordinator.

Visit www.teachingandmarking.com for more of my resources.

Contents

4.1.1.1 Energy Stores and Systems

1. What type of energy is stored in the following:
   a) A moving car.
   b) A parcel on a shelf.
   c) A stretched spring.
   d) An electric cell (battery).
   e) The nucleus of an atom
   f) A plate of rice.
   g) A lit Bunsen Burner.
   h) The siren on a fire engine.
   i) The power cables coming to your house.
   j) A lit barbecue

2. What energy changes take place when:
   a) A car rolls down a hill.
   b) A candle burns.
   c) A radio is playing a song.
   d) A spoon is dropped.
   e) A wind-up toy rabbit hops across the floor.
   f) An electric food mixer mixes soup.
   g) A singer uses a microphone.

3. Amy fits an arrow to a bow and pulls back the string.
   a) How is the energy now stored?
   She points the bow and arrow into the air and releases the string.
   b) How is the energy stored immediately after the arrow is released?
   As the arrow travels, the energy stored changes from one form to another.
   c) Describe this change.
   d) When the arrow reaches the top of its flight, how is the energy now stored?
   e) Describe the energy changes as the arrow falls.

4. Describe the energy changes in the following situations:
   a) The brakes are pressed in a moving train and it comes to rest in a station.
   b) A rocket burns fuel as it leaves the launchpad and heads for the moon.
   c) An electric kettle boils water.
   d) A sprinting rugby player is tackled by a member of the opposition.

5. Find a diagram and description of how electricity is generated in a coal burning power station. Describe the energy changes taking place in each part.

4.1.1.1 Energy Stores and Systems Answers

1
   a) Kinetic
   b) Gravitational Potential
   c) Elastic Potential
   d) Chemical
   e) Nuclear
   f) Chemical
   g) Thermal (heat)
   h) Sound
   i) Electrical
   j) Thermal (heat)

2
   a) Gravitational to Kinetic
   b) Chemical to Thermal (heat)
   c) Electrical to Sound
   d) Gravitational to Kinetic to Sound
   e) Elastic to Kinetic
   f) Electrical to Kinetic
   g) Sound to Electrical

3
   a) Elastic potential
   b) Kinetic
   c) Kinetic to Gravitational
   d) Gravitational
   e) Gravitational to Kinetic (to sound when it hits the ground)

4
   a) Kinetic to Sound and Thermal (heat)
   b) Chemical to Kinetic to Gravitational
   c) Electrical to Thermal (heat)
   d) Kinetic to Heat and Sound

5 Appropriately labelled and described diagram, beginning with a boiler, going through to the turbine and the generator

4.1.1.2 Changes in Energy

Kinetic Energy Calculations

Kinetic Energy = 0.5 x mass x (speed)^2

$E_K = \frac{1}{2} mv^2$

(Students should be able to recall and apply this equation.)

1. How much Kinetic Energy do the following bodies have (use the correct units each time):
   a) A 1 kg toy train travelling at 4 m/s.
   b) A 4 kg shot putt thrown at 2 m/s.
   c) A 50 kg cyclist on a 15 kg bike travelling at 9 m/s.
   d) A 600 kg car travelling at 20 m/s.
   e) A 10 000 kg train travelling at 25 m/s.
   f) A 200 g apple falling at 3 m/s.
   g) A 150 g bird flying at 12 m/s.
   h) A plane of mass 25 000 kg flying at 42 m/s.
   i) An arrow of mass 75 g flying at 35 m/s.
   j) A raindrop of mass 0.01 g falling at 15 m/s.

2. What is the mass of the following objects:
   a) A car travelling at 16 m/s which has 48000 J of Kinetic Energy.
   b) A cat running at 6 m/s which has 32.4 J of Kinetic Energy.
   c) A rock falling at 9 m/s which has 972 J of Kinetic Energy.
   d) A javelin thrown at 20 m/s which has 200 J of Kinetic Energy.
   e) A discus thrown at 18 m/s which has 324 J of Kinetic Energy.
   f) A frisbee thrown at 30 m/s which has 78.75 J of Kinetic Energy.
   g) A bullet travelling at 120 m/s which has 36 J of Kinetic Energy.
   h) A train travelling at 45 m/s which has 10.125 MJ of Kinetic Energy.
   i) A cyclist pedalling at 8 m/s who has 2.72 kJ of Kinetic Energy.
   j) A paper aeroplane flying at 1.7 m/s which has 3.6 mJ of Kinetic Energy.

3. Find the velocity (speed) of the following objects:
   a) A 1000 kg car with 12500 J of Kinetic Energy.
   b) A 2.6 kg skateboard with 20.8 J of Kinetic Energy.
   c) A 1.5 kg ferret with 6.75 J of Kinetic Energy.
   d) A 4 kg shot put with 200 J of Kinetic Energy
   e) A 50 g golf ball with 202.5 J of Kinetic Energy.
   f) A 180 kg motorbike with 12.96 kJ of Kinetic Energy.
   g) A 450 g football with 152.1 J of Kinetic Energy.
   h) A 140 000 kg blue whale with 2.52 MJ of Kinetic Energy.
   i) A 20 g dart with 3.24 J of Kinetic Energy.
   j) A 400 000 kg plane with 12.5 GJ of Kinetic Energy.

4. How much Kinetic Energy does Usain Bolt (mass 95 kg) have when he is running at 10 m/s?

5. A hummingbird is flying at 1.2 m/s. What is its kinetic energy if its mass is 2.8 g?

6

6. A black swan has a kinetic energy of 120 J when it is flying at 8 m/s. Find the mass of the swan.
7. A paintball has a kinetic energy of 0.49 J as it leaves the muzzle of the gun at 14 m/s. What is the mass of the paintball? (**give your answer in grams**)
8. The kinetic energy of a roller coaster truck is 16 000 J when it is travelling at 16 m/s. The truck has a mass of 100 kg and contains one person. What is the mass of the person?
9. A barrel of mass 80 kg has a kinetic energy of 1000 J as it rolls down a hill. How fast is it rolling?
10. A snooker ball of mass 160 g has a kinetic energy of 1.28 J. At what speed is it rolling?
11. A fully loaded Boeing 747 Jumbo jet has a mass of 400 000 kg. How fast is it flying when it has a kinetic energy of 980 MJ?
12. What speed must a motorcyclist attain to gain the same kinetic energy as a 1250 kg van travelling at 2 m/s if the combined mass of the motorcyclist and her bike is 200 kg?

Kinetic Energy Calculations Answers

1

    a) 8 J
    b) 8 J
    c) 2632.5 J
    d) 120000 J (120 kJ)
    e) 3125000 J (3.125 MJ)
    f) 0.9 J
    g) 10.8 J
    h) 22050000 J (22.05 MJ)
    i) 45.9375 J
    j) 0.001125 J or 1.125×10^{-3} J (1.125 mJ)

2

    a) 375 kg
    b) 1.8 kg
    c) 24 kg
    d) 1 kg
    e) 2 kg
    f) 175 g
    g) 5 g
    h) 10000 kg
    i) 85 kg
    j) 2.49 g (2 decimal places)

3

    a) 5 m/s
    b) 4 m/s
    c) 3 m/s
    d) 10 m/s
    e) 90 m/s
    f) 12 m/s
    g) 26 m/s
    h) 6 m/s
    i) 18 m/s
    j) 250 m/s

4.   4750 J
5.   2.016 J
6.   3.75 kg
7.   5g
8.   25 kg
9.   5 m/s
10.   4 m/s
11.   70 m/s
12.   5 m/s

Gravitational Potential Energy Calculations

G.P.E. = mass x gravitational field strength x height

$E_P = m\,g\,h$

(Students should be able to recall and apply this equation.)

(use g = 9.8 m/s² on the Earth)

1. How much Gravitational Potential Energy is gained in the following situations:
   a) An object of mass 10 kg lifted 2 m.
   b) An object of mass 8 kg lifted 5 m.
   c) An object of mass 12 kg lifted 6 m.
   d) An object of mass 6.5 kg lifted 0.75 m.
   e) An object of mass 15.25 kg lifted 4.8 m.
   f) An object of mass 250 g lifted 2 m.
   g) An object of mass 48 g lifted 50 cm.
   h) An object of mass 3500 g lifted 85 cm.
   i) An object of mass 75 g lifted 662 cm.
   j) An object of mass 924 g lifted 12 cm.

2. How much Gravitational Potential Energy is lost in the following situations:
   a) An object of mass 12 kg lowered 6 m
   b) An object of mass 250 g lowered 50 cm.
   c) An object of mass 8 kg lowered 60 cm
   d) An object of mass 480 g lowered 5 m.
   e) An object of mass 24 kg lowered 8 m
   f) An object of mass 2400 g lowered 520 cm.
   g) An object of mass 32 kg lowered 7.5 m
   h) An object of mass 45 g lowered 18 cm.
   i) An object of mass 0.660 kg lowered 0.6 m
   j) An object of mass 58 g lowered 14 m.

3. Through what height have the following objects moved:
   a) An object of mass 2 kg gaining 1200 J.
   b) An object of mass 1.8 kg losing 5600 J
   c) An object of mass 200 g gaining 196 J.
   d) An object of mass 25 kg losing 680 kJ
   e) An object of mass 500 kg gaining 450 MJ.
   f) An object of mass 680 g losing 820 J
   g) An object of mass 75 g gaining 18 J.
   h) An object of mass 5 g losing 64 J
   i) An object of mass 96 kg gaining 58 MJ.
   j) An object of mass 3.9 kg losing 7.4 kJ

4. What is the mass of the following:
   a) An object which gains 240 J when it is raised by 4 m.
   b) An object which loses 180 J when it is lowered by 2.5 m.
   c) An object which gains 720 J when it is raised by 8.4 m.

d) An object which loses 680 J when it is lowered by 9.2 m.
e) An object which gains 40 J when it is raised by 80cm.
f) An object which loses 18 J when it is lowered by 350 mm.
g) An object which gains 320 J when it is raised from 7 m to 12m
h) An object which loses 9.8 J when it is lowered from 7.62 m to 5.19m.
i) An object which gains 86 MJ when it is raised by 14 m.
j) An object which loses 56 kJ when it is lowered by 5.78 m.

5. Determine on which body in the Solar System the following energy changes took place (it is not possible to carry out or measure many of these changes for many reasons!):

Body	Gravitational Field Strength, g [N/kg]
Sun	274
Mercury	3.6
Venus	8.9
Moon	1.6
Mars	3.8
Jupiter	26
Saturn	11
Uranus	10.7
Neptune	14
Pluto	0.4

a) A 5 kg rock raised by 10 m gains 13700 J of E_p.
b) A rock (mass 12 kg) loses 1926 J of GPE when it falls 15 m.
c) A 480 kg space probe landing from a height of 6000 m loses 25.632 MJ of E_p.
d) A 160 kg spacecraft landing from a height of 5200 m loses 3.1616 MJ of GPE.
e) A diamond raindrop of mass 30 g loses 1950 J of Gravitational Potential Energy when it falls from a cloud 250 m above the surface of the planet.
f) A 250 kg space probe landing from a height of 1900 m loses 190 kJ of E_p.
g) A 358 kg spacecraft landing from a height of 2700 m loses 3479760 J of GPE.
h) A 60 kg space probe landing from a height of 3500m loses 2.94 MJ of GPE.
i) An astronaut of mass 75 kg climbs 2.8 m down the steps of his lander and his Gravitational Potential Energy changes by 336 J.
j) A rock (mass 500 kg) in orbit around this plant moves from 6 km above the surface to 5 km above the surface and loses 5.5 MJ of Gravitational Potential Energy.

6. How much energy does Jody (mass 45 kg) gain when she climbs a flight of stairs 3m high?

7. How much energy is stored in a Teddy Bear of mass 2.1 kg on a shelf 2.2m high?

8. How high does a climber (mass 55 kg) need to climb vertically up a climbing wall to gain 6000 J of Gravitational Potential Energy?
9. 18 kg of water falling over a waterfall loses 90 kJ of Gravitational Potential Energy. How high is the waterfall to the nearest metre?
10. An empty roller coaster carriage loses 120 kJ of energy as it goes from its highest to lowest point.
    a) Calculate the total mass of the carriage if the drop is 62 m.
    b) Explain the effect on the amount of Gravitational Potential Energy transferred if the carriage has four people in it.
    c) Determine the amount of Gravitational Potential Energy transferred if each of the four people in the carriage has a mass of 50 kg.
11. Bags of flour are added to a shelf 1.9 m high. How many 1.2 kg bags are required to make the Gravitational Potential Energy stored on the shelf greater than 300 J?
12. Charley says to Maddie "If I jump up 1.5 m and you jump down 1.2m, I will have gained as much Gravitational Potential Energy as you lost." If Charley has a mass of 48kg, what is the mass of Maddie?

Gravitational Potential Energy Calculations Answers

1
    a) 196 J
    b) 392 J
    c) 705.6 J
    d) 47.775 J
    e) 717.36 J
    f) 4.9 J
    g) 0.2352 J
    h) 29.155 J
    i) 4.8657 J
    j) 1.086624 J

2
    a) 705.6 J
    b) 1.225 J
    c) 47.04 J
    d) 23.52 J
    e) 1881.6 J
    f) 122.304 J
    g) 2352 J
    h) 0.07938 J
    i) 3.8808 J
    j) 7.9576 J

3 (answers to 2 dp where appropriate)
    a) 61.22 m (2dp)
    b) 317.46 m
    c) 100 m
    d) 2.78 m
    e) 91836 m
    f) 123.05 m
    g) 24.49 m
    h) 1306 m
    i) 61649 m
    j) 193.62 m

4
    a) 6.12 kg
    b) 7.35 kg
    c) 8.75 kg
    d) 7.54 kg
    e) 5.10 kg
    f) 5.25 kg
    g) 6.53 kg
    h) 0.41 kg
    i) 626822.16 kg
    j) 988.63 kg

5
    a) Sun
    b) Uranus
    c) Venus
    d) Mars
    e) Jupiter
    f) Pluto
    g) Mercury
    h) Neptune
    i) Moon
    j) Saturn

6   1323 J
7   45.279 J
8   11.13 m
10
    a) 197.5 kg
    b) Increase because there is more mass
    c) 241521 J
11   14 Bags
12   60kg

Elastic Potential Energy Calculations

Elastic Potential Energy = 0.5 x spring constant x (extension)^2

$E_e = \frac{1}{2} k e^2$

(Students should be able to apply this equation which is given on the Physics Equation Sheet.)

1. Calculate the amount of energy stored in each of the following springs:
    a) A spring with a spring constant of 85 N/m with an extension of 0.2 m
    b) A spring with a spring constant of 50 N/m with an extension of 0.45 m
    c) A spring with a spring constant of 26 N/m with an extension of 0.062 m
    d) A spring with a spring constant of 97 N/m with an extension of 0.048 m
    e) A spring with a spring constant of 6.1 N/m with an extension of 0.37 m
    f) A spring with a spring constant of 12.6 N/m with an extension of 3.6 cm
    g) A spring with a spring constant of 18.5 N/mm with an extension of 6.8 cm
    h) A spring with a spring constant of 59 N/cm with an extension of 55 cm
    i) A spring with a spring constant of 1600 N/m with an extension of 79 mm
    j) A spring with a spring constant of 7.5 N/mm with an extension of 92 mm

2. Determine the spring constant of the following springs:
    a) A spring which stores 2.7 J which has extended by 0.6m.
    b) A spring which stores 8.1 J which has extended by 0.9m.
    c) A spring which stores 3.456 J which has extended by 0.24m.
    d) A spring which stores 272 J which has extended by 0.8m.
    e) A spring which stores 172.8 J which has extended by 120 cm.
    f) A spring which stores 216.75 J which has extended by 85 cm.
    g) A spring which stores 2.2464 kJ which has extended by 2400 mm.
    h) A spring which stores 1.224 kJ which has extended by 360 cm.
    i) A spring which stores 26.912 kJ which has extended by 5800 mm.
    j) A spring which stores 1.0 MJ which has extended by 1250 m.

3. What is the extension of the following springs:
    a) A spring with a spring constant of 1000 N/m storing 20.8 J of Potential Energy.
    b) A spring with a spring constant of 1.5 N/m storing 6.75 J of Potential Energy.
    c) A spring with a spring constant of 4 N/m storing 200 J of Potential Energy
    d) A spring with a spring constant of 50 N/mm storing 202.5 J of Potential Energy.
    e) A spring with a spring constant of 180 N/m storing 12.96 kJ of Potential Energy.
    f) A spring with a spring constant of 140 000 N/m storing 2.52 MJ of Potential Energy.
    g) A spring with a spring constant of 20 N/mm storing 3.24 J of Potential Energy.
    h) A spring with a spring constant of 400 000 N/m storing 12.5 GJ of Potential Energy.

1

   a) 1.7 J
   b) 5.0625 J
   c) 0.04805 J
   d) 0.111744 J
   e) 0.417545 J
   f) 0.081648 J
   g) 42.772 J
   h) 892.375 J
   i) 4.9928 J
   j) 31.74 J

2

   a) 15 N/m
   b) 20 N/m
   c) 120 N/m
   d) 850 N/m
   e) 240 N/m
   f) 600 N/m
   g) 780 N/m
   h) 189 N/m
   i) 1600 N/m
   j) 1.28 N/m

3

   a) 0.204 m
   b) 3 m
   c) 10 m
   d) 2.85 m
   e) 12 m
   f) 6 m
   g) 0.018 m
   h) 250 m

Combined Energy Calculations
(use g = 9.8 m/s² for the Earth)

1. A large pendulum has a bob of mass 1.2 kg which is raised by 2.2 m.
   a) Find the gain in its Gravitational Potential Energy store.
   b) How much Kinetic Energy does it gain when it reaches the bottom? (Assume no energy is "lost")
   c) What is the maximum speed the bob reaches when it reaches the bottom?
2. An elastic band with a spring constant of 1240 N/m is stretched by 1.8 m.
   a) How much energy is stored in the elastic band?
   b) The elastic band is used to "fire" a ball bearing of mass 0.25 kg. How much Kinetic Energy will the ball bearing gain? (Assume no energy is "lost")
   c) What is the maximum velocity the ball bearing will reach?
3. An elastic band with a spring constant of 1600 N/m is stretched by 0.68m.
   a) How much energy is stored in the elastic band?
   b) The elastic band is used to "fire" a ball bearing of mass 0.01 kg. How much Gravitational Potential Energy will the ball bearing gain? (Assume no energy is "lost")
   c) What is the maximum height the ball bearing will reach?
4. A catapult is made using an elastic band with a spring constant of 360 N/m. It is used to fire a small ball of mass 45 g vertically into the air.
   a) If the elastic is stretched by 12 cm, how much energy does it store?
   b) Assuming no energy is "lost", how much Gravitational Potential Energy does the ball gain?
   c) What height will the ball reach?
   d) Assuming no energy is "lost" as the ball falls back to Earth, how much Kinetic Energy will the ball gain?
   e) What speed will the ball be travelling at when it hits the ground?
5. When a tennis ball of mass 60 g hits the floor at 5 m/s. How high will it bounce? (assume no energy is "lost").
6. A toy gun uses a stretched spring to fire a foam dart of mass 15 g at a target. If the dart is to stick to the target, it must have a speed of at least 4.5 m/s. If the spring has a spring constant of 66 N/m and it extends by 6 cm, will the dart stick to the target?
7. A roller coaster consists of 5 cars, each with a mass of 400 kg when fully loaded with people. The maximum drop on the ride is 60 m. Use this information to determine the fastest speed the ride can achieve.
   Extension. According to sources, "The Big One" in Blackpool, England, has a top speed of 74 miles per hour. Compare your answer to this. Is the answer you have for the above question a reasonable top speed for a roller coaster?
8. Shane says, "If I raise a bowling ball and a tennis ball to the same height, the bowling ball will gain more Gravitational Potential Energy, because it has more mass, so when I drop it, it will reach a faster speed than the tennis ball because it will gain more Kinetic Energy." Use the equations for Gravitational Potential Energy and Kinetic Energy to show that Shane is not correct.

1.
   a) 25.872 J
   b) 25.872 J
   c) 6.57 m/s (2 d.p.)

2.
   a) 2008.8 J
   b) 2008.8 J
   c) 126.77 m/s

3.
   a) 369.92 J
   b) 369.92 J
   c) 3774.69 m

4.
   a) 2.592 J
   b) 2.592 J
   c) 5.88 m
   d) 2.592 J
   e) 10.73 m/s

5. 1.28 m

6. Dart will not stick. 0.1188 J of E_e given to the dart. Dart needs 0.151875 J to stick.

7. Carriage gains 1176000 J of E_p. It will reach 34.29 m/s. 74 mph = 32.8 m/s. Therefore a reasonable answer.

8. Assuming no energy is lost mgh = $\frac{1}{2}$ mv². m can be cancelled from each side to give gh = $\frac{1}{2}$v². Therefore velocity is independent of mass.

4.1.1.3 Energy Changes in Systems (Also 4.3.2.2 Temperature Changes in a System and Specific Heat Capacity)

Specific Heat Calculations

Change in Thermal Energy = mass x specific heat capacity x temperature change

$$\Delta E = m\, c\, \Delta\theta$$

(Students should be able to apply this equation which is given on the Physics Equation Sheet.)

Substance	Specific Heat Capacity (c) J/kg°C
Water	4200
Aluminium	900
Iron	450
Ice	2100
Wood	1700
Copper	390
Lead	130
Glass	670
Air	718
Concrete	850

1. Calculate the change in Thermal Energy when:
   a) 2 kg of water increases temperature by 23°C.
   b) 3.5 kg of Aluminium decreases temperature by 12°C.
   c) 10 kg of Iron increases temperature by 50°C.
   d) 0.92 kg of Ice decreases temperature by 17°C.
   e) 6.4 kg of Wood increases temperature by 34°C.
   f) 4.1 kg of Copper increases temperature from 16°C to 35°C.
   g) 400 g of Lead decreases temperature from 73°C to 0°C.
   h) 18 kg of Glass decreases temperature from 14°C to 2°C.
   i) 0.025g of Air decreases temperature from 15°C to –18.
   j) 850 g of Concrete decreases temperature from -5°C to -26°C.

2. Find the mass:
   a) of Aluminium which requires 45000 J of energy to raise its temperature by 15°C.
   b) of Ice which requires 42000 J of energy to raise its temperature by 100°C.
   c) of Air which requires 2.154 kJ of energy to raise its temperature by 35°C.
   d) of Glass which requires 3.350 kJ of energy to raise its temperature from 16°C to 48°C.
   e) of Iron which requires 8.100 MJ of energy to raise its temperature from -22°C to 46°C.

f) of Concrete which emits 5950 J of energy when its temperature falls by 53°C.

g) of Wood which emits 51000 J of energy when its temperature falls by 66°C.

h) of Lead which emits 11.70 kJ of energy when its temperature falls by 31°C.

i) of Copper which emits 468 kJ of energy when its temperature falls from 58°C to -9°C.

j) of Water which emits 336 MJ of energy when its temperature falls from -5°C to -42°C.

3. Determine the specific heat capacity and use it to identify which material:
   a) Requires 21000 J of energy to raise the temperature of 2 kg of substance by 5°C.
   b) Requires 23205 J of energy to raise the temperature of 3.5 kg of substance by 17°C.
   c) Requires 579600 J of energy to raise the temperature of 14 kg of substance by 92°C.
   d) Requires 40052 J of energy to raise the temperature of 0.38 kg of substance by 62°C.
   e) Requires 25627.5 J of energy to raise the temperature of 750 g of substance by 51°C.
   f) Requires 129600 J of energy to raise the temperature of 8 kg of substance from 5°C to 23°C.
   g) Requires 790500 J of energy to raise the temperature of 62 kg of substance from 50°C to 65°C.
   h) Requires 25848 J of energy to raise the temperature of 0.23 kg of substance from 30°C to 150°C.
   i) Requires 15800.2 J of energy to raise the temperature of 590 g of substance from 4°C to 210°C.
   j) Requires 181440 J of energy to raise the temperature of 720 g of substance from -30°C to 30°C.

4. Determine the temperature change when:
   a) 5 kg of water absorbs 84000 J of heat energy.
   b) 12 kg of aluminium cools and gives out 24000 J of heat energy.
   c) 0.8 kg of lead absorbs 1040 J of heat energy.
   d) 26 kg of ice cools and gives out 54.6 kJ of heat energy.
   e) 0.98 kg of air cools and gives out 70.364 kJ of heat energy.
   f) 750 g of copper absorbs 23400 J of heat energy. What is the final temperature if the copper starts at 20 °C?
   g) 18 kg of iron absorbs 0.45 MJ of heat energy. What was the initial temperature of the water if the final temperature was 68 °C?
   h) 9 g of wood cools and gives out 56 mJ of heat energy.
   i) 16 kg of iron cools and gives out 75 MJ of heat energy.

Specific Heat Calculations Answers

3

1

a) 193200 J

b) 37800 J

c) 225000 J

d) 32844 J

e) 369920 J

f) 30381 J

g) 3796 J

h) 144720 J

i) 0.59235 J

j) 15172.5 J

a) Ice

b) Copper

c) Iron

d) Wood

e) Glass

f) Aluminium

g) Concrete

h) Air

i) Lead

j) Water

4

2

a) 3.33 kg

b) 0.2 kg

c) 0.0857 kg

d) 0.15625 kg

e) 264.71 kg

f) 0.132 kg

g) 0.4545 kg

h) 2.90 kg

i) 17.91 kg

j) 2162 kg

a) 4 °C

b) 2.22 °C

c) 2.89 °C

d) 1 °C

e) 100 °C

f) Change = 80 °C.
   Final temp = 100 °C

g) Change = 56 °C.
   Initial temp = 12 °C

h) 0.00366 °C

i) 10416 °C

4.1.1.4 Power

$$Power = \frac{energy\ transferred}{time}$$

$$Power = \frac{work\ done}{time}$$

(Students should be able to recall and apply these equations.)

1. Determine the Power when:
   a) Energy of 480 J is transferred in 24 s.
   b) Energy of 1500 J is transferred in 30 s.
   c) Energy of 96 J is transferred in 0.16 s.
   d) Energy of 840 J is transferred in 7 s.
   e) Energy of 390 J is transferred in 20 s.
   f) Energy of 68 kJ is transferred in 12 s.
   g) Energy of 12 MJ is transferred in 50 s.
   h) Energy of 750 kJ is transferred in 2.5 minutes.
   i) Energy of 160 GJ is transferred in 20 minutes.
   j) Energy of 360 MJ is transferred in 1 hour.
2. Calculate the Power when:
   a) 500 J of Work is done in 25 s.
   b) 2500 J of Work is done in 5 s.
   c) 1024 J of Work is done in 16 s.
   d) 360 J of Work is done in 18 s.
   e) 4800 J of Work is done in 40 s.
   f) 76 kJ of Work is done in 152 s.
   g) 18 J of Work is done in 20 ms.
   h) 16 MJ of Work is done in 8 minutes.
   i) 90 kJ of Work is done in 12 minutes.
   j) 2400 MJ of Work is done in 2 hours.
3. Calculate the Energy Transferred when:
   a) Power of 30 W is exerted for 5 s.
   b) Power of 40 W is exerted for 7 s.
   c) Power of 160 W is exerted for 25 s.
   d) Power of 250 W is exerted for 80 s.
   e) Power of 960 W is exerted for 150 s.
   f) Power of 12 W is exerted for 1 minute.
   g) Power of 42 kW is exerted for 64 s.
   h) Power of 84 kW is exerted for 2 minutes.
   i) Power of 75 MW is exerted for 15 minutes.
   j) Power of 56 mW is exerted for 5 hours.
4. What is the Work Done when:
   a) Power of 75 W is exerted for 2 s.
   b) Power of 53 W is exerted for 15 s.

c) Power of 180 W is exerted for 28 s.

d) Power of 620 W is exerted for 90 s.

e) Power of 850 W is exerted for 200 s.

f) Power of 20 W is exerted for 6 minutes.

g) Power of 4 kW is exerted for 80 s.

h) Power of 36 kW is exerted for 9 minutes.

i) Power of 47 MW is exerted for 22 minutes.

j) Power of 90 mW is exerted for 7 hours.

5. Find the Time taken for: *(In these questions, convert the answers to the most suitable units of time)*

a) A device with a Power of 4 W transfers 36 J of Energy.

b) A device with a Power of 15 W does 750 J of Work.

c) A device with a Power of 150 W transfers 9000 J of Energy.

d) A device with a Power of 20 W does 500 J of Work.

e) A device with a Power of 60 W transfers 15 kJ of Energy.

f) A device with a Power of 90 kW does 8.1 MJ of Work.

g) A device with a Power of 8.7 MW transfers 280 MJ of Energy.

h) A device with a Power of 12 MW does 640 kJ of Work.

i) A device with a Power of 75 mW transfers 22.5 J of Energy.

j) A device with a Power of 32 W does 16 MJ of Work.

6a) Find the work done on a car with Power of 8000 W in a time of 7.3 s

b) Find the work done on a body with Power of 100 W in a time of 2 s

c) Calculate the work done on a vehicle with Power of 6000 W in a time of 3.4 s

d) Calculate the time taken for a car to do work of 600 J when its Power is 1000 W

e) Determine the work done on a car with Power of 100 W in a time of 2.3 s

f) Determine the time taken for a body to do work of 7000 J when its Power is 800 W

g) Calculate the time taken for a body to do work of 3000 J when its Power is 5000 W

h) Determine the work done on a vehicle with Power of 700 W in a time of 4.1 s

i) Find the Power of a car in a time of 6.5 s when the energy transferred is 4000 J

j) Determine the time taken for a body to do work of 200 J when its Power is 200 W

4.1.1.4 Power Answers

1

- a) 20 W
- b) 50 W
- c) 600 W
- d) 120 W
- e) 19.5 W
- f) 5666 W
- g) 240000 W
- h) 5000 W
- i) 133333333 W
- j) 100000 W

2

- a) 20 W
- b) 500 W
- c) 64 W
- d) 20 W
- e) 120 W
- f) 500 W
- g) 900 W
- h) 33333 W
- i) 125 W
- j) 333333 W

3

- a) 150 J
- b) 280 J
- c) 4000 J
- d) 20000 J
- e) 144000 J
- f) 720 J
- g) 2688000 J
- h) 10080000 J
- i) 6.75×10^{10} J
- j) 1008 J

4

- a) 150 J
- b) 795 J
- c) 5040 J
- d) 55800 J
- e) 170000 J
- f) 7200 J
- g) 320000 J
- h) 19440000 J
- i) 6.204×10^{10} J
- j) 2268 J

5

- a) 9 s
- b) 50 s
- c) 60 s = 1 minute
- d) 25 s
- e) 250 s = 4.17 minutes
      = 4 minutes 10s
- f) 90 s = 1.5 minutes
- g) 32.18 s
- h) 0.053 s
- i) 300 s = 5 minutes
- j) 500000 s = 8333.3 minutes
  = 138.88 hours = 5.787 days
  = 5 days 18 hours 53 minutes 20s

6

- a) 58000 J
- b) 200 J
- c) 20000 J
- d) 0.6 s
- e) 230 J
- f) 8.8 s
- g) 0.6 s
- h) 2900 J
- i) 620 W
- j) 1 s

4.1.2.1 Energy Transfers in a System

1. What is the Law of Conservation of Energy?
2. A Pendulum bob is raised 0.1 m and then released so it swings evenly. The mass of the bob is 0.5 kg.
   a) How much Gravitational Potential Energy does the bob have before it is released? ($g = 9.8$ m/s^2)
   b) How much Gravitational Potential Energy does the bob have at the bottom of the swing?
   c) How much Kinetic Energy will the bob have at the bottom of the swing? (assume air resistance is zero)
   d) When the bob has 0.3 J of Gravitational Potential Energy, how much Kinetic Energy does it have?
   e) When the bob has 0.1 J of Kinetic Energy, how much Gravitational Potential Energy does it have?
3. A skateboarder of mass 60 kg stands at the top of a half-pipe which is 3m high.
   a) How much Gravitational Potential Energy does he have? ($g = 9.8$ m/s^2)
   b) How much Gravitational Potential Energy will he have at the bottom of the half-pipe?
   c) How much Kinetic Energy will he have at the bottom of the half-pipe? (assume air resistance and friction are zero)
   d) When the skateboarder has 1000J of Gravitational Potential Energy, how much Kinetic Energy does it have?
   e) When the skateboarder has 800J of Kinetic Energy, how much Gravitational Potential Energy does it have?
4. A cyclist of mass 85 kg pedals to the top of a hill 32 m high. ($g = 9.8$ m/s^2)
   a) How much Gravitational Potential Energy does she have?
   b) She then rolls down to the bottom of the hill. How much Kinetic Energy will she gain when she gets to the bottom?
   c) In fact, she only gains 20000 J. Explain what has happened to the remaining energy.
5. A car's petrol tank is filled with petrol which stores 125000 J of chemical energy.
   a) If all of the fuel is converted to Kinetic Energy, how much Kinetic Energy will the car have?
   b) If the car drives to the top of a hill, what energy will it gain?
   c) How much of this energy will it have?
   d) In practice, it is impossible for the car to convert all of the fuel energy into Kinetic Energy. Explain into what other forms this energy is converted.

4.1.2.1 Energy Transfers in a System Answers

1. Energy cannot be created or destroyed only converted from one form to another.

2
   a) 0.49 J
   b) 0 J
   c) 0.49 J
   d) 0.19 J
   e) 0.39 J

3
   a) 1764 J
   b) 0 J
   c) 1764 J
   d) 764 J
   e) 964 J

4
   a) 26656 J
   b) 26656 J
   c) "Lost"/ Dissipated as sound and heat

5
   a) 125000 J
   b) GPE/E_p
   c) 125000 J
   d) "Lost"/ Dissipated as sound and heat

4.1.2.2 Efficiency

$$\text{Efficiency} = \frac{useful\ output\ energy\ transfer}{total\ input\ energy\ transfer}$$

$$\text{Efficiency} = \frac{useful\ power\ output}{total\ power\ input}$$

(Students should be able to recall and apply these equations.)

1. Calculate the Efficiency of a device with:
   a) a useful output energy transfer of 12 J and a total input energy transfer of 18 J.
   b) a useful output energy transfer of 350 J and a total input energy transfer of 1750 J.
   c) a useful output energy transfer of 0.92 J and a total input energy transfer of 5.48 J.
   d) a useful output energy transfer of 63 kJ and a total input energy transfer of 84780 J.
   e) a useful output energy transfer of 29 kJ and a total input energy transfer of 2.32 MJ.
   f) a total input energy transfer of 60 J and a useful output energy transfer of 15 J.
   g) a total input energy transfer of 590 J and a useful output energy transfer of 118 J.
   h) a total input energy transfer of 0.9 J and a useful output energy transfer of 675 mJ.
   i) a total input energy transfer of 9.75 kJ and a useful output energy transfer of 246 J.
   j) a total input energy transfer of 0.72 MJ and a useful output energy transfer of 53 kJ.

2. Find the Useful Output Energy Transferred by a device with:
   a) a total input energy transfer of 1250 J and an efficiency of 0.30
   b) a total input energy transfer of 60 J and an efficiency of 15%
   c) a total input energy transfer of 1800 J and an efficiency of 0.95
   d) a total input energy transfer of 36 kJ and an efficiency of 42%
   e) a total input energy transfer of 540 mJ and an efficiency of 0.08
   f) a total input energy transfer of 0.76 MJ and an efficiency of 5%
   g) a total input energy transfer of 0.28 J and an efficiency of 0.72
   h) a total input energy transfer of 0.09 kJ and an efficiency of 37%
   i) a total input energy transfer of 4.8 MJ and an efficiency of 0.64
   j) a total input energy transfer of 820 kJ and an efficiency of 25%

3. Determine the Total Input Energy:
   a) a useful output energy transfer of 1250 J and an efficiency of 0.30
   b) a useful output energy transfer of 60 J and an efficiency of 15%
   c) a useful output energy transfer of 1800 J and an efficiency of 0.95
   d) a useful output energy transfer of 36 J and an efficiency of 42%
   e) a useful output energy transfer of 540 mJ and an efficiency of 0.08.
   f) a useful output energy transfer of 0.76 MJ and an efficiency of 5%

g) a useful output energy transfer of 0.28 J and an efficiency of 0.72.

h) a useful output energy transfer of 0.09 kJ and an efficiency of 37%

i) a useful output energy transfer of 4.8M J and an efficiency of 0.64.

j) a useful output energy transfer of 820 kJ and an efficiency of 25%

4. Find the Efficiency:

a) a useful power output of 2 W and a total power input energy of 10 W.

b) a useful power output of 15 W and a total power input energy of 80 W.

c) a useful power output of 38 W and a total power input energy of 73 W.

d) a useful power output of 460 W and a total power input energy of 940 W.

e) a useful power output of 80 kW and a total power input energy of 660 kW.

f) a useful power output of 59 W and a total power input energy of 6 kW.

g) a useful power output of 4 MW and a total power input energy of 25 MW.

h) a useful power output of 28 kW and a total power input energy of 5 MW.

i) a useful power output of 770 mW and a total power input energy of 33 W.

j) a useful power output of 195 mW and a total power input energy of 4 kW.

5. Determine the Useful Power Output:

a) a total power input of 80 W and an efficiency of 0.40

b) a total power input of 96 W and an efficiency of 12.5%

c) a total power input of 3400 W and an efficiency of 0.65

d) a total power input of 36 kW and an efficiency of 24%

e) a total power input of 408 kW and an efficiency of 0.75

f) a total power input of 79 MW and an efficiency of 5%

g) a total power input of 280 MW and an efficiency of 0.9

h) a total power input of 550 mW and an efficiency of 65%

i) a total power input of 1250 mW and an efficiency of 0.08

j) a total power input of 640 GW and an efficiency of 3.4%

6. Calculate the Total Power Input:

a) a useful power output of 2500 W and an efficiency of 0.80

b) a useful power output of 640 W and an efficiency of 35%

c) a useful power output of 76 kW and an efficiency of 0.44

d) a useful power output of 190 kW and an efficiency of 22.5%

e) a useful power output of 580 mW and an efficiency of 0.74

f) a useful power output of 960 mW and an efficiency of 90%

g) a useful power output of 84 MW and an efficiency of 0.52

h) a useful power output of 0.36 MW and an efficiency of 60%

i) a useful power output of 4 GW and an efficiency of 0.05

j) a useful power output of 360 GW and an efficiency of 0.04%

7. An engineer takes measurements which show that the light energy emitted by a bulb is 32 Joules each second and the heat emitted by the same bulb is 38 Joules each second. When she measures the input power to the bulb, she finds that it is 60 Watts. Use a calculation to explain that she has made a mistake and must repeat her experiment.

4.1.2.2 Efficiency Answers (accept % for efficiency in all answers)

1

a) 0.66
b) 0.20
c) 0.17
d) 0.74
e) 0.0125
f) 0.25
g) 0.20
h) 0.75
i) 0.025
j) 0.074

2

a) 375 J
b) 9 J
c) 1710 J
d) 15.12 J
e) 43.2 mJ
f) 0.038 MJ
g) 0.2016 J
h) 0.0333 kJ
i) 3.072 MJ
j) 205 kJ

3

a) 4167 J
b) 400 J
c) 1895 J
d) 85.71 J
e) 6750 mJ
f) 15.2 J
g) 0.39 J
h) 0.243 kJ
i) 7.5 MJ

4

a) 0.2
b) 0.1875
c) 0.52
d) 0.489
e) 0.12
f) 0.00983
g) 0.16
h) 0.0056
i) 0.023
j) 0.00004875

5

a) 32 W
b) 12 W
c) 2210 W
d) 8.64 kW
e) 306 kW
f) 3.95 MW
g) 252 MW
h) 357.5 mW
i) 100 mW
j) 21.76 GW

6

a) 3125 W
b) 1828.57 W
c) 172.72 kW
d) 844.4 kW
e) 783.78 mW
f) 1066.7 mW
g) 161.54 MW
h) 0.6 MW
i) 80 GW
j) 9000 GW

7) 32 + 38 = 70 J/s which is greater than the input of 60 W

1. What is the meaning of the word "renewable" in the context of energy?
2. Make a list of 4 non-renewable energy resources.
3. Make a list of 5 renewable energy resources.
4. What do we mean by "energy dense"? Explain with examples and comparisons.
5. What do we mean by a "reliable source of energy"? Explain with examples and comparisons.
6. What is meant by the terms "commissioning and "decommissioning"? Explain with examples and comparisons.
7. Give 2 advantages and 2 disadvantages of generating electricity using fossil fuels.
8. Give 2 advantages and 2 disadvantages of generating electricity using the Sun.
9. Give 2 advantages and 2 disadvantages of generating electricity using the wind.
10. Give 2 advantages and 2 disadvantages of generating electricity using waves.
11. Give 2 advantages and 2 disadvantages of generating electricity using the tides.
12. Give 2 advantages and 2 disadvantages of generating electricity using geothermal energy.
13. Give 2 advantages and 2 disadvantages of generating electricity using biofuels.
14. Give 2 advantages and 2 disadvantages of generating electricity using nuclear fuels.
15. Give 2 advantages and 2 disadvantages of generating electricity using hydro-electric plants.

4.1.3 National and Global Energy Resources Answers

1. A renewable energy resource is one that is being (or can be) replenished as it is used.
2. Coal, Oil, Gas, Nuclear
3. Biofuel, Wind, Wave, Solar, Geothermal, Tidal, Hydro
4. A lot of energy from a small amount of fuel or resource. Coal is energy dense. 1 kg of coal will burn for hours and release a lot of heat energy which can then be transferred to other energy stores. Wind is not energy dense. A lot of wind is needed to turn a turbine.
5. Reliable energy sources are ones which are there all of the time and not intermittent. Gas is reliable. As long as it is present, it can be burned to release heat. The Sun is unreliable as it is dependent both on weather conditions and the time of day.
6. Commissioning means setting up (a power plant) and decommissioning means dismantling (a power plant). Nuclear power has high commissioning and decommissioning costs as plants have high safety standards and can take many tens of years to dismantle and clear a former nuclear site. A gas plant by comparison can be set up and removed very quickly. The same with solar panels.
7. Fossil fuels are energy dense, reliable, readily available, relatively cheap, etc.
   Fossil fuels produce Carbon Dioxide, acid rain, non-renewable, etc
8. Solar power is cheap, no Carbon dioxide, non-polluting, etc
   Solar unreliable, does not work at night, inefficient (currently), etc
9. Wind power is cheap, no Carbon dioxide, non-polluting, etc
   Wind power is unreliable, noisy, eyesore, inefficient, etc
10. Wave power is cheap, no Carbon dioxide, non-polluting, etc
    Wave power untested, unreliable, damages habitats (tidal), etc
11. Geothermal is no Carbon dioxide, non-polluting, etc
    Geothermal is location specific, can damage environments, etc
12. Biofuels are Carbon Neutral, renewable, etc
13. Biofuels use land that could be used for food crops, still produce Carbon Dioxide, etc
14. Nuclear fuels release no carbon dioxide, energy dense, reliable, etc.
    Nuclear have high commissioning and decommissioning costs, produce nuclear waste, etc
15. Hydro-electrics are reliable, carbon dioxide free, etc
    Hydro-electrics only work in certain locations, damage environment, etc

4.2.1.1 Standard Circuit Diagram Symbols

1. Draw the correct circuit symbols for the following components:
   a) Cell
   b) Battery
   c) Open Switch
   d) Closed Switch
   e) Lamp (bulb)
   f) Fuse
   g) Resistor
   h) Variable Resistor
   i) Thermistor
   j) Light Dependent Resistor
   k) Diode
   l) Light Emitting Diode
   m) Ammeter
   n) Voltmeter
2. Draw a circuit diagram with 2 lamps.
3. Draw a circuit diagram with 2 lamps and one switch which switches them both on and off.
4. Draw a circuit diagram with 2 lamps with a switch for each lamp.
5. Draw a circuit diagram showing how you could measure the current through a lamp.
6. Draw a circuit diagram showing how you could measure the potential difference across a diode.
7. Draw a circuit diagram showing how you could vary the current through a light emitting diode.
8. Draw a circuit diagram showing how you could vary the current through a resistor and measure both the current through the resistor and the potential difference across the resistor at the same time.

1.

a) ⊣⊢ cell

b) ⊣|----|⊢ battery

c) switch (open)

d) switch (closed)

e) lamp

f) fuse

g) resistor

h) variable resistor

i) thermistor

j) LDR

k) diode

l) LED

m) ammeter

n) voltmeter

2. Suitable series or parallel circuit
3. Suitable series circuit with switch in series with 2 lamps
4. Suitable parallel circuit with switch on each branch

5. Suitable circuit with ammeter in series with a lamp
6. Suitable circuit with a voltmeter in parallel with a diode.
7. Suitable circuit with a variable resistor in series with an LED
8. Suitable diagram of the simple test circuit measuring the pd across and current through a resistor.

4.2.1.2 Electrical charge and current

Charge Flow = current x time

$$Q = I \, t$$

(Students should be able to recall and apply this equation.)

1. Find the Charge Transferred when:
   a) A current of 6 A flows for 15 s.
   b) A current of 14 A flows for 30 s.
   c) A current of 2 A flows for 240 s.
   d) A current of 20 A flows for 180 s.
   e) A current of 0.8 A flows for 2 minutes.
   f) A current of 0.09 A flows for 42 minutes.
   g) A current of 75 mA flows for 55 minutes.
   h) A current of 14 kA flows for 39 s.
   i) A current of 0.065 kA flows for 2 hours.
   j) A current of 2 MA flows for 0.75 hours.
2. Calculate the Current that flows when:
   a) 16 C of charge is transferred in 8 s.
   b) 84 C of charge is transferred in 14 s.
   c) 5.5 C of charge is transferred in 11 s.
   d) 120 C of charge is transferred in 30 s.
   e) 0.76 C of charge is transferred in 1.9 s.
   f) 3 kC of charge is transferred in 5 minutes.
   g) 480 mC of charge is transferred in 3 minutes.
   h) 0.96 C of charge is transferred in 0.8minutes.
   i) 60 MC of charge is transferred in 24 hours.
   j) 220 mC of charge is transferred in 11 ms.
3. Determine the Time taken for:
   (In these questions, convert the answers to the most suitable units of time)
   a) 45 C of charge to be transferred by a current of 5 A
   b) 64 C of charge to be transferred by a current of 8 A
   c) 126 C of charge to be transferred by a current of 12 A
   d) 950 C of charge to be transferred by a current of 4 A
   e) 3 C of charge to be transferred by a current of 0.02 A
   f) 56 kC of charge to be transferred by a current of 7 A
   g) 32 mC of charge to be transferred by a current of 0.8 mA
   h) 860 MC of charge to be transferred by a current of 7.5 kA
   i) 0.25 C of charge to be transferred by a current of 1.75 mA
   j) 102 kC of charge to be transferred by a current of 4 mA

4a) Find the charge passing through a length of wire when a current of 1.1 A flows for 0.7 s

b) Determine the time taken for a current of 9.4 A to move a charge of 4.8 C

c) Find the charge passing through a length of wire when a current of 3.2 A flows for 5.2 s

d) Determine the current which flows when a charge of 1.2 C is moved in 7.5 s

e) Find the current which flows when a charge of 7.2 C is moved in 9 s

f) Find the time taken for a current of 1.9 A to move a charge of 8.2 C

g) Calculate the time taken for a current of 5 A to move a charge of 6.8 C

h) Calculate the current which flows when a charge of 1.3 is moved in 5 s

i) Calculate the current which flows when a charge of 9.2 C is moved in 4 s

j) Determine the current which flows when a charge of 5.9 C is moved in 8.9 s

1

a) 90 C
b) 420 C
c) 480 C
d) 3600 C
e) 96 C
f) 226.8 C
g) 247.5 C
h) 546000 C
i) 468000 C
j) 5.4 x10⁹ C

2

a) 2 A
b) 6 A
c) 0.5 A
d) 4 A
e) 0.4 A
f) 10 A
g) 0.0027 A
h) 0.02 A
i) 694 A
j) 20 A

3

a) 9 s
b) 8 s
c) 10.5 s
d) 237.5 s
e) 150 s
f) 8000 s = 133.33minutes
   = 2hours 13 mins 20s
g) 4 s
h) 114666 s = 1911 minutes
   = 31 hours 51 minutes 7 s
i) 142.86 s = 2 minutes 23 s
j) 25500000 s = 425000 minutes = 7083 hours = 295 days 3 hours 20 minutes

4

a) 0.77 C
b) 0.51 s
c) 17 C
d) 0.16 A
e) 0.8 A
f) 4.3 s
g) 1.4 s
h) 0.26 A
i) 2.3 A
j) 0.66 A

4.2.1.3 Current, Resistance and Potential Difference

Potential Difference = current × resistance
$$V = I R$$
(Students should be able to recall and apply this equation.)

1. Determine the Potential Difference across:
   a) A Resistance of 60 Ω when a current of 5 A is passing through it.
   b) A Resistance of 120 Ω when a current of 40 A is passing through it.
   c) A Resistance of 75 Ω when a current of 20 A is passing through it.
   d) A Resistance of 34 kΩ when a current of 6.8 A is passing through it.
   e) A Resistance of 280 mΩ when a current of 0.32 A is passing through it.
   f) A Resistance of 440 kΩ when a current of 9 mA is passing through it.
   g) A Resistance of 0.85 MΩ when a current of 17 kA is passing through it.
   h) A Resistance of 900 kΩ when a current of 850 mA is passing through it.
   i) A Resistance of 3 GΩ when a current of 0.45 mA is passing through it.
   j) A Resistance of 5.7 MΩ when a current of 7.7 µA is passing through it.

2. Calculate the Current that flows through:
   a) A Resistance of 8 Ω which has a potential difference of 24 V across it.
   b) A Resistance of 3 Ω which has a potential difference of 42 V across it.
   c) A Resistance of 9.2 kΩ which has a potential difference of 184 kV across it.
   d) A Resistance of 560 kΩ which has a potential difference of 1440 kV across it.
   e) A Resistance of 62 MΩ which has a potential difference of 31 MV across it.
   f) A Resistance of 280 MΩ which has a potential difference of 70 MV across it.
   g) A Resistance of 760 mΩ which has a potential difference of 1600 mV across it.
   h) A Resistance of 49 mΩ which has a potential difference of 0.539 V across it.
   i) A Resistance of 12.8 MΩ which has a potential difference of 930 kV across it.
   j) A Resistance of 0.075 kΩ which has a potential difference of 8.2 MV across it.

3. Find the Resistance when:
   a) A Current of 2 A flows through a resistance which has a Potential Difference of 36 V across it.
   b) A Current of 1.5 A flows through a resistance which has a Potential Difference of 52.5 V across it.
   c) A Current of 5.9 kA flows through a resistance which has a Potential Difference of 108 kV across it.
   d) A Current of 340 kA flows through a resistance which has a Potential Difference of 850 kV across it.
   e) A Current of 4 MA flows through a resistance which has a Potential Difference of 560 MV across it.
   f) A Current of 690 GA flows through a resistance which has a Potential Difference of 330 GV across it.
   g) A Current of 790 mA flows through a resistance which has a Potential Difference of 1185 mV across it.
   h) A Current of 32 MA flows through a resistance which has a Potential Difference of

4.80 GV across it.

i) A Current of 8400 mA flows through a resistance which has a Potential Difference of 64 V across it.

j) A Current of 9.2 kA flows through a resistance which has a Potential Difference of 2750 MV across it.

4a) Find the current through a component with a potential difference of 9.4 V and a resistance of 7.4 Ω

b) Determine the resistance of a resistor with a current of 6.2 A and a potential difference of 3 V

c) Determine the current through a resistor with a potential difference of 8.8 V and a resistance of 1.8 Ω

d) Calculate the potential difference across a length of wire with a current of 1 A and a resistance of 1.5 Ω

e) Find the potential difference across a length of wire with a current of 3.1 A and a resistance of 9.9 Ω

f) Calculate the resistance of a length of wire with a current of 1.4 A and a potential difference of 0.3 V

g) Calculate the resistance of a component with a current of 8 A and a potential difference of 1.3 V

h) Find the current through a resistor with a potential difference of 9.2 V and a resistance of 0.2 Ω

i) Find the potential difference across a resistor with a current of 9.5 A and a resistance of 0.4 Ω

j) Calculate the current through a resistor with a potential difference of 1.9 V and a resistance of 1.1 Ω

1

    a) 300 V
    b) 4800 V
    c) 1500 V
    d) 2312 V
    e) 0.0896 V
    f) 3960 V
    g) 14.45 GV
    h) 765 kV
    i) 1.35 MV
    j) 43.89 V

3

    a) 18 Ω
    b) 35 Ω
    c) 18.3 Ω
    d) 2.5 Ω
    e) 140 Ω
    f) 0.478 Ω
    g) 1.5 Ω
    h) 150 Ω
    i) 7.62 Ω
    j) 299 kΩ

2

    a) 3 A
    b) 14 A
    c) 20 A
    d) 2.57 A
    e) 0.5 A
    f) 0.25 A
    g) 2.11 A
    h) 11 A
    i) 0.073 A
    j) 109 A

4

    a) 1.3 A
    b) 0.48 Ω
    c) 4.9 A
    d) 1.5 V
    e) 31 V
    f) 0.21 Ω
    g) 0.16 Ω
    h) 46 A
    i) 3.8 V
    j) 1.7 A

4.2.1.4 Resistors

1. What is the circuit symbol for a resistor?
2. What does a resistor do in a circuit?
3. Sketch a graph showing the relationship between the current and potential difference for a resistor.
4. What is the circuit symbol for a thermistor?
5. Explain how the resistance of a thermistor changes as the temperature changes.
6. Draw a sketch graph to show how the resistance of a thermistor changes as the temperature increases.
7. Describe how a thermistor can be used as a thermostat in an oven.
8. What is the circuit symbol for a Light Dependent Resistor?
9. Explain how the resistance of a Light Dependent Resistor changes as the light intensity changes.
10. Draw a sketch graph to show how the resistance of a Light Dependent Resistor changes as the light intensity increases.
11. Describe how a Light Dependent Resistor can be used as a control for street lighting.
12. Draw a circuit diagram to show the use of an LDR to control street lighting.
13. What is the circuit symbol for a lamp?
14. What is meant by a "filament lamp"?
15. Sketch a graph showing the relationship between the current and potential difference for a filament lamp.
16. Describe how and why the resistance changes as the filament gets hotter and use these ideas to explain the shape of the graph you have just drawn.
17. What is the circuit symbol for a diode?
18. What does a diode do?
19. Sketch a graph showing the relationship between the current and potential difference for a diode.
20. Use your ideas of what a diode does to explain the shape of the graph you have just drawn.
21. Draw a circuit diagram using the correct circuit symbols of the circuit you could use to obtain the graphs you have sketched in questions 3, 15 and 19. Explain the roles of the components you have drawn.

4.2.1.4 Resistors Answers

1.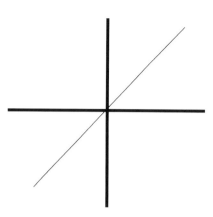
2. Reduces the current
3.

4.
5. As the temperature increases, the resistance decreases
6.

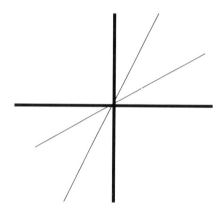

7. The thermistor could be placed inside the oven. As the oven temperature increased, the resistance of the thermistor would decrease. The thermistor should be connected in series with a second resistor and in parallel with the heater. The decrease in resistance of the thermistor will cause the potential difference across it to fall, causing a drop in potential difference across the heater. This will switch off the heater. As the temperature falls, the resistance of the thermistor rises, the potential difference across it rises as does the potential difference across the heater so it switches on again.

8.
9. As the light intensity increases, the resistance of the LDR decreases.

10.

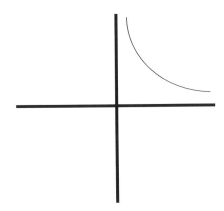

11. The LDR could be placed inside the street light. As the light intensity increased, the resistance of the LDR would decrease. The LDR should be connected in series with a second resistor and in parallel with the bulb. The decrease in resistance of the LDR will cause the potential difference across it to fall, causing a drop in potential difference across the bulb. This will switch off the bulb. As the light intensity falls, the resistance of the LDR rises, the potential difference across it rises as does the potential difference across the bulb so it switches on again.

12. Suitable diagram with an LDR and a bulb.

13.

14. A bulb in which a thin wire has a current passing through it. As the wire gets hotter, it glows, giving out light.

15.

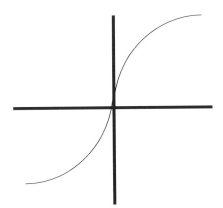

16. As the current increases, the wire gets hotter. This causes an increase in resistance as there are more collisions of electrons in the wire. Therefore a greater potential difference is required to produce a higher current.

17.

18. Allows current to pass through in one direction only. Prevents current flowing in the opposite direction.

19.

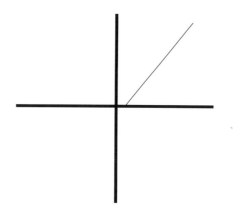

20. The diode only lets the current flow in one direction. When the polarity is reversed, no current flows.

21. Suitable diagram of a simple test circuit with explanation of each component.

4.2.2 Series and Parallel Circuits

$$R_{TOTAL} = R_1 + R_2$$

1. Determine the total resistance in the following arrangements:

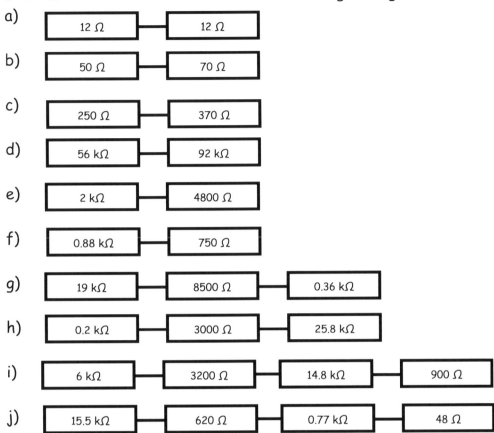

a) | 12 Ω | | 12 Ω |

b) | 50 Ω | | 70 Ω |

c) | 250 Ω | | 370 Ω |

d) | 56 kΩ | | 92 kΩ |

e) | 2 kΩ | | 4800 Ω |

f) | 0.88 kΩ | | 750 Ω |

g) | 19 kΩ | | 8500 Ω | | 0.36 kΩ |

h) | 0.2 kΩ | | 3000 Ω | | 25.8 kΩ |

i) | 6 kΩ | | 3200 Ω | | 14.8 kΩ | | 900 Ω |

j) | 15.5 kΩ | | 620 Ω | | 0.77 kΩ | | 48 Ω |

2. Look at the diagram below
    a) Is meter A an ammeter or a voltmeter?
    b) What is the reading on meter A? Include the units.
    c) Is meter A an ammeter or a voltmeter?
    d) What is the reading on meter B? Include the units.

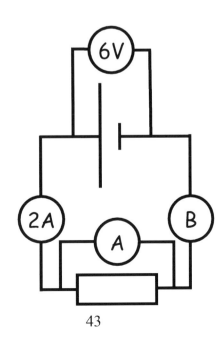

3. Look at the diagram below
   a) Is meter C an ammeter or a voltmeter?
   b) What is the reading on meter C? Include the units.
   c) Is meter D an ammeter or a voltmeter?
   d) What is the reading on meter D? Include the units.
   e) Is meter E an ammeter or a voltmeter?
   f) What is the reading on meter E? Include the units.

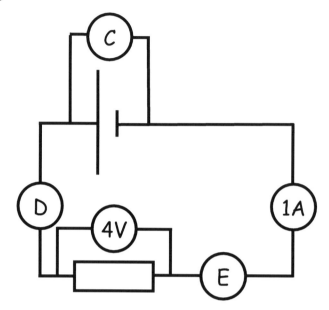

4. Look at the diagram below. All of the resistors are identical.
   a) Is meter F an ammeter or a voltmeter?
   b) What is the reading on meter F? Include the units.
   c) Is meter G an ammeter or a voltmeter?
   d) What is the reading on meter G? Include the units.
   e) Is meter H an ammeter or a voltmeter?
   f) What is the reading on meter H? Include the units.

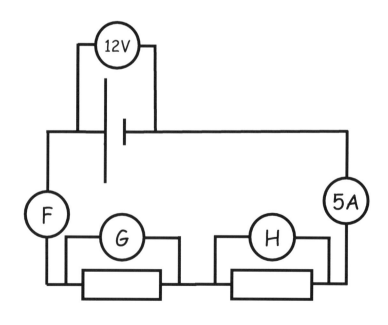

5. Look at the diagram below. All of the resistors are identical.
   a) Is meter I an ammeter or a voltmeter?
   b) What is the reading on meter I? Include the units.
   c) Is meter J an ammeter or a voltmeter?
   d) What is the reading on meter J? Include the units.
   e) Is meter K an ammeter or a voltmeter?
   f) What is the reading on meter K? Include the units.
   g) Is meter L an ammeter or a voltmeter?
   h) What is the reading on meter L? Include the units.
   i) Is meter M an ammeter or a voltmeter?
   j) What is the reading on meter M? Include the units.
   k) Is meter N an ammeter or a voltmeter?
   l) What is the reading on meter N? Include the units.

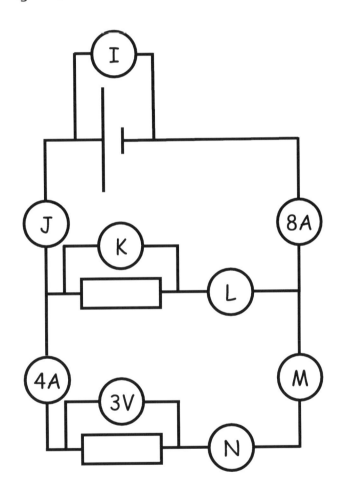

6. Look at the diagram below. All of the resistors are identical.
   a) Is meter P an ammeter or a voltmeter?
   b) What is the reading on meter P? Include the units.
   c) Is meter Q an ammeter or a voltmeter?
   d) What is the reading on meter Q? Include the units.
   e) Is meter R an ammeter or a voltmeter?
   f) What is the reading on meter R? Include the units.
   g) Is meter S an ammeter or a voltmeter?
   h) What is the reading on meter S? Include the units.

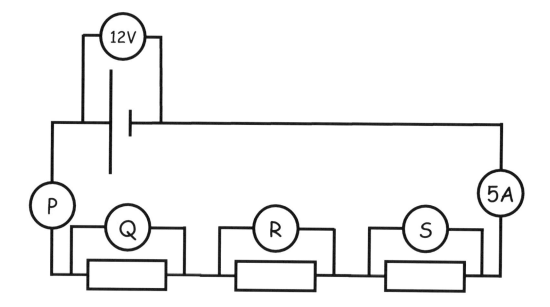

7. Look at the diagram below. All of the resistors are identical.
   a) Is meter T an ammeter or a voltmeter?
   b) What is the reading on meter T? Include the units.
   c) Is meter U an ammeter or a voltmeter?
   d) What is the reading on meter U? Include the units.
   e) Is meter W an ammeter or a voltmeter?
   f) What is the reading on meter W? Include the units.
   g) Is meter X an ammeter or a voltmeter?
   h) What is the reading on meter X? Include the units.
   i) Is meter Y an ammeter or a voltmeter?
   j) What is the reading on meter Y? Include the units.

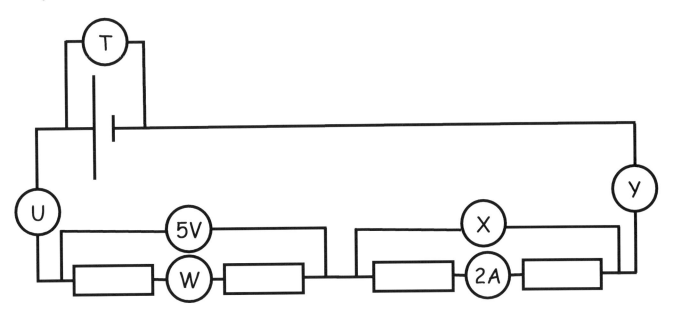

4.2.2 Series and Parallel Circuits Answers

1.
   a) 24 Ω
   b) 120 Ω
   c) 620 Ω
   d) 148 Ω
   e) 6800 Ω
   f) 1630 Ω
   g) 27860 Ω
   h) 29000 Ω
   i) 24900 Ω
   j) 16938 Ω

A. Voltmeter 6V
B. Ammeter 2A
C. Voltmeter 4V
D. Ammeter 1A
E. Ammeter 1A
F. Ammeter 5A
G. Voltmeter 6V
H. Voltmeter 6V
I. Voltmeter 3V
J. Ammeter 8A
K. Voltmeter 3V
L. Ammeter 4A
M. Ammeter 4A
N. Ammeter 4A
P. Ammeter 5A
Q. Voltmeter 4V
R. Voltmeter 4V
S. Voltmeter 4V
T. Voltmeter 10V
U. Ammeter 2A
W. Ammeter 2A
X. Voltmeter 5V
Y. Ammeter 2A

4.2.3 Direct and Alternating Potential Difference and Mains electricity

1. What does DC stand for?
2. Describe what happens in a DC circuit.
3. Give an example of a simple DC circuit.
4. What does AC stand for?
5. Describe what happens in an AC circuit.
6. Give an example of a simple AC circuit.
7. What is the frequency of the UK mains supply?
8. What is the potential difference of the UK mains supply?
9. An oscilloscope is a device that can be used to show a visual representation of an electric current. Sketch what would be seen if:
   a) The oscilloscope is connected to a DC supply
   b) The oscilloscope is connected to an AC supply
10. Explain how the oscilloscope trace can be used to determine:
    a) The potential difference of the supply.
    b) The frequency of an AC supply
11. What is the colour of the live wire in a three-pin plug?
12. What is the job of the live wire?
13. What is the colour of the neutral wire in a three-pin plug?
14. What is the job of the neutral wire?
15. What is the colour of the earth wire in a three-pin plug?
16. What is the job of the earth wire?
17. Explain 5 safety features of the three-pin plug.
18. A Residual Current Device is used to determine if there is a potential difference between the live and earth wires and breaks the circuit if there is none. Explain why this is an important safety feature.
19. Explain why a live wire may be dangerous even when a switch in the mains circuit is open.

4.2.3 Direct and Alternating Potential Difference and Mains Electricity Answers

1. Direct Current
2. The polarity is constant
3. A simple torch, etc. or Suitable diagram.
4. Alternating current
5. The polarity changes regularly (eg 50 times per second)
6. Household electricity, etc
7. 50 Hz
8. 230 V
9. a) 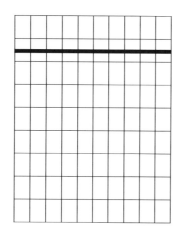 b)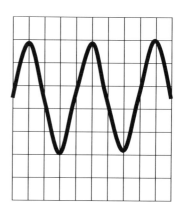

10.
   a) Measure the height of the waveform.
   b) Measure the wavelength of the wave to determine the time period and then take the reciprocal of the answer.
11. Brown
12. The current enters the device through the live wire
13. Blue
14. The current leaves the device through the neutral wire
15. Yellow and Green striped
16. If there is a fault and the case of the device becomes live, the earth wire provides a route for the current to flow to earth so that the current does not pass through a person who touches the device. At this point, the fuse should blow.
17. Cable grip, Fuse, Earth wire, Insulating plastic case, Insulating sections on brass pins
18. The RCCB determines if there is a difference in electrical potential between the live and neutral wires. In the event of the cable being cut and the wires coming into contact, the RCCB "trips" causing the current to be switched off and the device thus becoming safe.
19. Even if the switch is off, there could be a fault or a power surge of some kind. The switch could be faulty and displaying off when it is on. Etc

4.2.4.1 Electrical Power

Power = potential difference x current

$$P = V I$$

Power = (current)² x resistance

$$P = I^2 R$$

(Students should be able to recall and apply these equations.)

1. Calculate the Power when:
   a) A Current of 6 A flows due to a Potential Difference of 5 V.
   b) A Current of 15 A flows due to a Potential Difference of 9 V.
   c) A Current of 35 mA flows due to a Potential Difference of 10 V.
   d) A Current of 20 A flows due to a Potential Difference of 75 kV.
   e) A Current of 95 mA flows due to a Potential Difference of 84 kV.
   f) A Current of 3 A flows through a device with a Resistance of 6 Ω.
   g) A Current of 0.5 A flows through a device with a Resistance of 2500 Ω.
   h) A Current of 15 mA flows through a device with a Resistance of 75 Ω.
   i) A Current of 450 mA flows through a device with a Resistance of 900 kΩ.
   j) A Current of 620 mA flows through a device with a Resistance of 820 MΩ.

2. Determine the Potential Difference across:
   a) A device with a Power of 16 W with a Current of 2 A passing through it.
   b) A device with a Power of 27 W with a Current of 3 A passing through it.
   c) A device with a Power of 3.8 W with a Current of 0.1 A passing through it.
   d) A device with a Power of 490 W with a Current of 0.75 A passing through it.
   e) A device with a Power of 9 kW with a Current of 30 A passing through it.
   f) A device with a Power of 84 W with a Current of 12 mA passing through it.
   g) A device with a Power of 500 MW with a Current of 40 A passing through it.
   h) A device with a Power of 900 MW with a Current of 0.15 kA passing through it.
   i) A device with a Power of 64 W with a Current of 7.2 A passing through it.
   j) A device with a Power of 0.69 kW with a Current of 590 mA passing through it.

3. Find the Current passing through:
   a) A device with a Power of 24 W with a Potential Difference of 3 V across it.
   b) A device with a Power of 27 W with a Resistance of 3 Ω.
   c) A device with a Power of 56 W with a Potential Difference of 7 V across it.
   d) A device with a Power of 1728 W with a Resistance of 12 Ω.
   e) A device with a Power of 9.4 kW with a Potential Difference of 230 V across it.
   f) A device with a Power of 67 kW with a Resistance of 4500 Ω.
   g) A device with a Power of 1500 W with a Potential Difference of 0.42 kV across it.
   h) A device with a Power of 8.64 MW with a Resistance of 100 kΩ.
   i) A device with a Power of 600 mW with a Potential Difference of 4.5 V across it.
   j) A device with a Power of 58 MW with a Resistance of 820 kΩ.

4. Calculate the Resistance of:
   a) A device with a Power of 16 W with a Current of 2 A passing through it.
   b) A device with a Power of 52 W with a Current of 1 A passing through it.

c) A device with a Power of 4.9 kW with a Current of 0.7 kA passing through it.
d) A device with a Power of 35 kW with a Current of 5 kA passing through it.
e) A device with a Power of 680 mW with a Current of 12 mA passing through it.
f) A device with a Power of 10.8 mW with a Current of 0.9 mA passing through it.
g) A device with a Power of 750 MW with a Current of 25 MA passing through it.
h) A device with a Power of 2.8 GW with a Current of 1.5 MA passing through it.
i) A device with a Power of 900 MW with a Current of 450 A passing through it.
j) A device with a Power of 24 W with a Current of 36 mA passing through it.

4.2.4.1 Electrical Power Answers

1

a) 30 W
b) 135 W
c) 0.35 W
d) 1.5 MW
e) 7980 W
f) 54 W
g) 625 W
h) 0.016875 W
i) 182250 W
j) 315 MW

2

a) 8 V
b) 9 V
c) 38 V
d) 653 V
e) 300 V
f) 7000 V
g) 12.5 MV
h) 6 MV
i) 8.9 V
j) 1169 V

3

a) 8 A
b) 3 A
c) 8 A
d) 12 A
e) 40.87A
f) 3.86 A
g) 3571 A
h) 9.3 A
i) 0.13 A
j) 8.41 A

4

a) 4 Ω
b) 52 Ω
c) 10 Ω
d) 104 mΩ
e) 4722 Ω
f) 13333 Ω
g) 1.2 $\mu\Omega$
h) 1.2 mΩ
i) 4444 Ω
j) 18519 Ω

4.2.4.2 Energy transfers in everyday appliances

Energy Transferred = power x time
$$E = P\,t$$
Energy Transferred = charge flow x potential differences
$$E = Q\,V$$
(Students should be able to recall and apply these equations.)

1. Calculate the Energy Transferred when:
   a) A device with a Power of 15 W is switched on for 12 s.
   b) A device with a Power of 45 W is switched on for 9 s.
   c) A device with a Power of 520 W is switched on for 45 s.
   d) A device with a Power of 98000 W is switched on for 140 s.
   e) A device with a Power of 64 kW is switched on for 8 minutes.
   f) A device with a Power of 3600 kW is switched on for 15 minutes.
   g) A device with a Power of 85 MW is switched on for 7 minutes.
   h) A device with a Power of 7200 MW is switched on for 3 hours.
   i) A device with a Power of 91 mW is switched on for 2 seconds.
   j) A device with a Power of 250 mW is switched on for 4 hours.

2. Determine the Power when:
   a) 20 J of Energy are transferred in 4 s.
   b) 972 J of Energy are transferred in 30 s.
   c) 3400 J of Energy are transferred in 72 s.
   d) 0.13 J of Energy are transferred in 26 s.
   e) 1600 mJ of Energy are transferred in 4 minutes.
   f) 830 mJ of Energy are transferred in 8 s.
   g) 760 kJ of Energy are transferred in 2 minutes.
   h) 450 MJ of Energy are transferred in 7 minutes.
   i) 69 GJ of Energy are transferred in 5 hours.
   j) 530 nJ of Energy are transferred in 5 s.

3. Find the Time taken for:
   a) A device with a Power of 3 W to transfer 12 J of energy.
   b) A device with a Power of 6 W to transfer 46 J of energy.
   c) A device with a Power of 40 W to transfer 6200 J of energy.
   d) A device with a Power of 125 W to transfer 845 kJ of energy.
   e) A device with a Power of 1.8 kW to transfer 950 kJ of energy.
   f) A device with a Power of 590 kW to transfer 830 MJ of energy.
   g) A device with a Power of 92 MW to transfer 7600 GJ of energy.
   h) A device with a Power of 7.8 GW to transfer 3.9 GJ of energy.
   i) A device with a Power of 800 mW to transfer 20 J of energy.
   j) A device with a Power of 2700 kW to transfer 8.1 MJ of energy.

4. Determine the Energy Transferred when:
   a) A Charge of 7 C is caused to flow by a Potential Difference of 6 V.
   b) A Charge of 39 C is caused to flow by a Potential Difference of 80 V.

c) A Charge of 710 mC is caused to flow by a Potential Difference of 230 V.

d) A Charge of 80 MC is caused to flow by a Potential Difference of 140 mV.

e) A Charge of 240 mC is caused to flow by a Potential Difference of 700 kV.

f) A Charge of 51 kC is caused to flow by a Potential Difference of 6 kV.

g) A Charge of 6.5 MC is caused to flow by a Potential Difference of 55 V.

h) A Charge of 4300 C is caused to flow by a Potential Difference of 960 mV.

i) A Charge of 9.40 GC is caused to flow by a Potential Difference of 2.8 mV.

j) A Charge of 61 kC is caused to flow by a Potential Difference of 48 kV.

5. Calculate the Charge that flows when:

a) 48 J of energy is transferred by a potential difference of 8 V.

b) 550 J of energy is transferred by a potential difference of 25 V.

c) 63000 J of energy is transferred by a potential difference of 140 V.

d) 3.9 kJ of energy is transferred by a potential difference of 6.5 V.

e) 870 kJ of energy is transferred by a potential difference of 55 kV.

f) 7.6 MJ of energy is transferred by a potential difference of 480 kV.

g) 912 MJ of energy is transferred by a potential difference of 30 MV.

h) 0.32 GJ of energy is transferred by a potential difference of 16 kV.

i) 155 mJ of energy is transferred by a potential difference of 0.05 V.

j) 2400 mJ of energy is transferred by a potential difference of 3.6 kV.

6. Find the Potential Difference when:

a) 88 J of energy is transferred as 11 C of charge flows.

b) 465 J of energy is transferred as 15 C of charge flows.

c) 5600 J of energy is transferred as 11.2 C of charge flows.

d) 0.69 J of energy is transferred as 0.9 C of charge flows.

e) 0.78 kJ of energy is transferred as 3.9 C of charge flows.

f) 99 kJ of energy is transferred as 50 C of charge flows.

g) 3600 kJ of energy is transferred as 12.5 kC of charge flows.

h) 2.4 MJ of energy is transferred as 64 kC of charge flows.

i) 100 mJ of energy is transferred as 0.02 C of charge flows.

j) 760 GJ of energy is transferred as 1.9 GC of charge flows.

1
a) 180 J
b) 405 J
c) 23400 J
d) 13.72 MJ
e) 30.72 MJ
f) 3.24 GJ
g) 35.7 GJ
h) 77076 TJ
i) 0.182 J
j) 3600 J

2
a) 5 W
b) 32.4 W
c) 47.2 W
d) 5 mW
e) 6.7 mW
f) 0.10375 W
g) 6.3 W
h) 1.071 MW
i) 3.833 MW
j) 106 nW

3
a) 4 s
b) 7.67 s
c) 155 s
d) 6760 s
e) 528 s
f) 1407 s
g) 82609 s
h) 0.5 s
i) 25 s
j) 3 s

4
a) 42 J
b) 3120 J
c) 163.3 J
d) 11.2 MJ
e) 700 kJ
f) 306 MJ
g) 357.5 MJ
h) 4128 J
i) 26.32 MJ
j) 2.928 GJ

5
a) 6 C
b) 22 C
c) 450 C
d) 600 C
e) 15.818 C
f) 15833 C
g) 30.4 C
h) 20000 C
i) 3.1 C
j) 667 μC

6
a) 8 V
b) 31 V
c) 500 V
d) 0.77 V
e) 200 V
f) 1980 V
g) 288 V
h) 37.5 V
i) 5 V
j) 400 V

4.2.4.3 The National Grid

1. What is the National Grid and what does it do?
2. Make a list of the main components of the National Grid.
3. What is a Step-Up Transformer?
4. To approximately what value is the potential difference stepped up?
5. Where is the potential difference stepped up?
6. Why is the potential difference stepped up in the National Grid?
7. What is a Step-Down Transformer?
8. Where is the potential difference stepped down?
9. To approximately what value is the potential difference stepped down?
10. Why is the potential difference stepped down in the National Grid?
11. The National Grid sometimes uses above-ground pylons to transfer electricity.
    a) Explain 1 advantage of using above-ground pylons to transmit electricity.
    b) Explain 1 disadvantage of using above-ground pylons to transmit electricity.
12. The National Grid sometimes uses buried cables to transfer electricity.
    a) Explain 1 advantage of using buried cables to transmit electricity.
    b) Explain 1 disadvantage of using buried cables to transmit electricity.
13. Before the National Grid was in operation, local areas generated their own electricity and distributed it locally.
    a) Explain the advantages of this system.
    b) Explain the disadvantages of this system.

4.2.4.3 The National Grid Answers

1. The National Grid is a system of cables and transformers linking power stations to consumers.
2. Power stations, Pylons, Transformers, Power Lines, etc
3. A transformer which increases the potential difference and decreases the current
4. 400000V
5. Step up transformers at the power stations
6. To reduces loses due to heating of the wire
7. A transformer which decreases the potential difference and increases the current
8. Before homes and businesses (after the transmission wires)
9. 230V for domestic use. Higher for industrial and businesses
10. For safety in our homes.
11.
    a) They are easy to access for maintenance and are kept cool by wind, etc
    b) They are an eyesore and dangerous for low flying aircraft, parachutists, etc
12.
    a) They are out of the way, invisible and "safe"
    b) Difficult to access, stay warm, etc
13.
    a) There was less transfer of energy, local demands met locally, etc
    b) If the local supply failed then the whole town went down.

4.2.5.1 Static charge (Physics Only)

1. What is the charge on the following sub-atomic particles:
   a) A Proton
   b) An Electron
   c) A Neutron
2. Whereabouts in the atom are the following sub-atomic particles:
   a) A Proton
   b) An Electron
   c) A Neutron
3. When an insulator is rubbed, which particle is transferred?
4. If a material gains electrons, what will the charge on it be?
5. If a material loses electrons, what will the charge on it be?
6. When an insulator is rubbed, it can become charged. When a conductor is rubbed, it usually does not become charged. Explain this observation.
7. When a nylon rod is rubbed with a silk cloth, the nylon becomes positively charged and the silk cloth becomes negatively charged. Explain these observations in terms of electron transfer.
8. A car driver experiences a shock when she touches the door of the car as she exits it after a journey. Explain why this happens.
9. The Van Der Graaf Generator is a safe way to show the discharge of static electricity.
   a) Explain how the first dome becomes charged.
   b) The second dome is connected to earth. Explain why.
   c) Explain why we see a spark after a period of time.
   d) A boy with long hair places both hands onto the first sphere and the sphere is charged. Explain why his hair stands up.
10. A nylon rod is rubbed with a cloth and hung in a cradle which is free to rotate. A second nylon rod is rubbed with a cloth and moved close to the first rod. (NB – nylon gains a negative charge when rubbed with a cloth)
    a) What will be observed?
    b) Explain this observation.
11. A nylon rod is rubbed with a cloth and hung in a cradle which is free to rotate. An acetate rod is rubbed with a cloth and moved close to the first rod. (NB – acetate gains a positive charge when rubbed with a cloth)
    a) What will be observed?
    b) Explain this observation.

4.2.5.1 Static charge (Physics Only) Answers

1.
   a) +1
   b) –1
   c) 0

2.
   a) Nucleus
   b) Orbits/Orbitals/Shells
   c) Nucleus

3. Electron
4. Negative
5. Positive
6. The insulator retails the charge because the charge cannot flow though it. The charge is static. The conductor allows charge to flow therefore does not retain the charge (unless it is isolated).
7. The nylon rod loses electrons to the silk cloth, OWTTE
8. The driver moves on the seat, transferring electrons between herself and the seat. She becomes charged. As she leaves the car, she touches the metal body of the car which conducts electrons away from (or onto) her. As the electrons jump, she feels the "shock".

9.
   a) The rubber/plastic belt rubs a metal comb. Electrons are transferred to the belt and carried up to the dome. A second comb rubs the electrons off the belt and conduct the electrons to the isolated dome. The dome is now negatively charged.
   b) The electrons from the first dome will jump to the second so that they can and spread over the nearest large object. This is the earth.
   c) The electrons spread over the boy. Each her becomes negative. The negative charges repel each other so each hair moves away from the other.

10.
   a) The rods will move away from each other
   b) Each rod is negatively charged. Like charges repel. Therefore the rods move apart.

11.
   a) The rods will move towards each other
   b) The rods are oppositely charged. Opposite charges attract. Therefore the rods move together.

4.2.5.2 Electric fields (Physics Only)

1. Define an "electric field".
2. Where is a field the strongest?
3. When drawing arrows to show the direction of an electric field, in which direction do they always point?
4. Draw a proton and show the electric field around it.
5. A second proton is placed near to the first proton. Explain, in terms of the electric field, what will happen to the second proton.
6. An electron is placed near to the first proton. Explain, in terms of the electric field, what will happen to the electron.
7. Draw an electron and show the electric field around it.
8. Draw a neutron and show the electric field around it.
9. What happens to the strength of the electric field:
   a) as the distance from the charged particle increases?
   b) as the distance from the charged particle decreases?
10. vv

4.2.5.2 Electric fields (Physics Only) Answers

1. A region of influence where forces are experienced
2. Closer to the charged object
3. Positive to negative
4. Diagram with a centre circle with at least 8 arrows pointing away from the centre of the circle, evenly spaced by eye.
5. The electric field from the two protons will interact causing the protons to repel each other.
6. The electric field from the proton and the electron will interact causing the particles to attract each other.
7. Diagram with a centre circle with at least 8 arrows pointing towards the centre of the circle, evenly spaced by eye.
8. A circle with no arrows. No field lines.
9.
     a. The strength of the field decreases
     b. The strength of the field increases

4.3.1 Density of Materials (Including Changes of State)

$$\text{Density} = \frac{\text{mass}}{\text{volume}}$$

$$\rho = \frac{m}{V}$$

(Students should be able to recall and apply this equation.)

1. Sketch a diagram of the arrangements of particles in:
   a) A solid
   b) A liquid
   c) A gas
2. Describe the motion of particles in:
   a) A solid
   b) A liquid
   c) A gas
3. Name the following changes of state:
   a) Solid to Liquid
   b) Liquid to Solid
   c) Liquid to Gas
   d) Gas to Liquid
   e) Solid to Gas (and vice versa)
4. A substance has a melting point of -17 C and a boiling point of 84 C. In what state is the substance at:
   a) -28 C
   b) -13 C
   c) 25 C
   d) 149 C
5. A substance has a melting point of -102 C and a boiling point of -45 C. In what state is the substance at:
   a) -149 C
   b) -28 C
   c) -13 C
   d) -95 C
6. Changes of state are physical changes and not chemical changes. Use your knowledge of physical and chemical changes to explain this statement.
7. 120 g of water are heated until it all boils. What is the mass of steam created?
8. A glass of coke (mass 260 g) has 40 g of ice added to it and then it is left in the sun. When all of the ice has melted, what is the total mass of the glass and liquid?
9. Which state of matter has the greatest density? Explain your answer.
10. Which state of matter has the least density? Explain your answer.
11. Calculate the density of the following objects. Give your answer in appropriate units:
    a) An object with a mass of 100 kg and a volume of 10 m^3.
    b) An object with a mass of 64 kg and a volume of 8 m^3.

c) An object with a mass of 12.5 kg and a volume of 2.5 m³.
d) An object with a mass of 520 kg and a volume of 30 m³.
e) An object with a mass of 7800 kg and a volume of 1.3 m³.
f) An object with a mass of 4.5 kg and a volume of 0.9 m³.
g) An object with a mass of 3.6 kg and a volume of 0.04 m³.
h) An object with a mass of 2 tonnes and a volume of 250 m³.
i) An object with a mass of 8100 g and a volume of 108 c m³.
j) An object with a mass of 90 g and a volume of 5 c m³.

12. Find the mass of the following objects:
    a) An object with a volume of 10 m³ and a density of 10 kg/m³.
    b) An object with a volume of 16 m³ and a density of 4 kg/m³.
    c) An object with a volume of 7 m³ and a density of 12 kg/m³.
    d) An object with a volume of 9.1 m³ and a density of 20 kg/m³.
    e) An object with a volume of 24 m³ and a density of 6.25 kg/m³.
    f) An object with a volume of 300 m³ and a density of 88 kg/m³.
    g) An object with a volume of 42000 cm³ and a density of 2.5 kg/m³.
    h) An object with a volume of 0.06 m³ and a density of 0.35 kg/cm³.
    i) An object with a volume of 530 cm³ and a density of 140 g/cm³.
    j) An object with a volume of 68 cm³ and a density of 1500 g/m³.

13. Determine the volume of the following objects:
    a) An object with a mass of 120 kg and a density of 10 kg/m³.
    b) An object with a mass of 64 kg and a density of 8 kg/m³.
    c) An object with a mass of 720 kg and a density of 15 kg/m³.
    d) An object with a mass of 8.4 kg and a density of 0.35 kg/m³.
    e) An object with a mass of 9600 kg and a density of 42 kg/m³.
    f) An object with a mass of 0.55 kg and a density of 1.1 kg/m³.
    g) An object with a mass of 2400 g and a density of 30 kg/m³.
    h) An object with a mass of 3.5 kg and a density of 700 g/m³.
    i) An object with a mass of 4.8 kg and a density of 0.01 kg/cm³.
    j) An object with a mass of 520 g and a density of 1.3 g/cm³.

14a) Find the density of an object with a mass of 8.6 kg and a volume of 8.3 m³
b) Determine the mass of an object with a density of 1 kg/m³ and a volume of 9.4 m³
c) Calculate the mass of an object with a density of 7.2 kg/m³ and a volume of 6.5 m³
d) Determine the volume of an object with a mass of 4.5 kg and a density of 3.9 kg/m³
e) Determine the density of an irregular object with a mass of 1 kg and a volume of 5.8 m³
f) Find the density of an object with a mass of 1.1 kg and a volume of 9.6 m³
g) Find the volume of a body with a mass of 3.5 kg and a density of 7.8 kg/m³
h) Determine the volume of a body with a mass of 7.4 kg and a density of 8 kg/m³
i) Find the mass of a body with a density of 4.6 kg/m³ and a volume of 1 m³
j) Find the density of an object with a mass of 2.4 kg and a volume of 5 m³

1. a) Suitable diagram
   b) Suitable diagram
   c) Suitable diagram

2.
   a) Vibrating about a fixed position, etc
   b) Moving but still in contact. Greater distance than solids, etc
   c) Free movement, etc

3.
   a) Melting
   b) Freezing
   c) Boiling/Evaporation
   d) Condensation
   e) Sublimation

4.
   a) Solid
   b) Liquid
   c) Liquid
   d) Gas

5.
   a) Solid
   b) Gas
   c) Gas
   d) Liquid

6. They are reversible
7. 120g
8. 300g
9. Solid. Particles packed closest
10. Gas. Particles least closely packed
11.
   a) 10 kg/m^3
   b) 8 kg/m^3
   c) 5 kg/m^3

   d) 17.3 kg/m^3
   e) 6000 kg/m^3
   f) 5 kg/m^3
   g) 90 kg/m^3
   h) 8 kg/m^3
   i) 75 g/cm^3 = 75000 kg/m^3
   j) 18 g/cm^3 = 18000 kg/m^3

12.
   a) 100 kg
   b) 64 kg
   c) 84 kg
   d) 182 kg
   e) 150 kg
   f) 26400 kg
   g) 0.105 kg = 105 g
   h) 21000 kg
   i) 74200 g = 74.2 kg
   j) 0.102 g

13.
   a) 12 m^3
   b) 8 m^3
   c) 48 m^3
   d) 24 m^3
   e) 228.6 m^3
   f) 0.5 m^3
   g) 0.08 m^3
   h) 5 m^3
   i) 480 cm^3
   j) 400 cm^3

14
   a) 1 kg/m^3
   b) 9.4 kg
   c) 47 kg
   d) 1.2 m^3
   e) 0.17 kg/m^3
   f) 0.11 kg/m^3
   g) 0.45 m^3
   h) 0.93 m^3
   i) 4.6 kg
   j) 0.48 kg/m^3

4.3.2.1 Internal Energy

1. Sketch a diagram of the particles inside a:
   a) Solid
   b) Liquid
   c) Gas
2. Which of the states has the particles with the greatest energy? Explain why.
3. Which of the states has the particles with the least energy? Explain why.
4. Write down 4 words which describe changes of state and the changes they describe.
5. A solid is heated. What happens in terms of particles?
6. Define the "Internal Energy" of a system.
7. How can the Internal energy of a system be increased? Describe what happens to the particles in this case.
8. How can the Internal energy of a system be decreased? Describe what happens to the particles in this case.
9. When heated, the particles in a substance undergo changes. Describe, in detail, the changes the particles in a solid undergo until the substance becomes a liquid and then a gas.
10. When cooled, the particles in a substance undergo changes. Describe, in detail, the changes the particles in a gas undergo until the substance becomes a liquid and then a solid.

4.3.2.1 Internal Energy Answers

1.
    a) Suitable Diagram – regular, close packed particles
    b) Suitable Diagram – irregular, close packed particles
    c) Suitable Diagram – randomly, widely spaced particles
2. Gas. Particles moving fastest
3. Solid. Particles moving slowest
4. Solid to Liquid – Melting
   Liquid to Solid - Freezing
   Liquid to Gas – Boiling/Evaporation
   Gas to Liquid - Condensation
   Solid to Gas (and vice versa) - Sublimation
5. Particles gain more energy. Vibrate faster and further until bonds break. Liquid forms.
6. The internal energy is the total amount of kinetic energy and potential energy of all the particles in a system.
7. Heat it up. Particles gain more kinetic energy.
8. Cool it down. Particles lose kinetic energy
9. In a solid the particles are held together tightly and vibrating about a fixed position. As the temperature increases, the distance between the particles increases, the strong bonds are broken and the particles, now in a liquid state, are free to flow over and around each other. As the temperature continues to increase, the particles gain further energy, enough to escape from the surface of the liquid. They now have enough energy to move quickly in all directions with no forces of attraction between particles.
10. Reverse of above.

4.3.2.3 Changes of Heat and Specific Latent Heat

Energy for a Change of State = mass x specific latent heat

$$E = m L$$

(Students should be able to apply this equation which is given on the Physics Equation Sheet.)

Substance	Specific Latent Heat of Fusion J/kg	Specific Latent Heat of Vapourisation J/kg
Aluminium	66000	400000
Ethanol	110000	860000
Carbon Dioxide	180000	570000
Gold	1100000	64000
Lead	25000	870000
Water	340000	2300000

1. Determine the Energy Change:
   a) When 2 kg of Aluminium melts.
   b) When 16 kg of Gold melts.
   c) When 0.8 kg of Lead melts.
   d) When 0.45 kg of Water freezes.
   e) When 6.8 kg of Ethanol freezes.
   f) When 10 kg of Aluminium boils.
   g) When 0.65 kg of Carbon Dioxide boils.
   h) When 125 g of Water boils.
   i) When 920g of Ethanol condenses.
   j) When 28g of Gold condenses.

2. Calculate the mass:
   a) Of Aluminium which takes in 192000 J of energy when it melts.
   b) Of Water which takes in 560000 J of energy when it melts.
   c) Of Lead which takes in 10 kJ of energy when it melts.
   d) Of Gold which gives out 55 kJ of energy when it freezes.
   e) Of Ethanol which gives out 75 MJ of energy when it freezes.
   f) Of Carbon Dioxide which takes in 5130000 J of energy when it evaporates.
   g) Of Aluminium which takes in 1 MJ of energy when it evaporates.
   h) Of Gold which gives out 256 kJ of energy when it condenses.
   i) Of Lead which gives out 29 kJ of energy when it condenses.
   j) Of Water which gives out 8.5 MJ of energy when it condenses.

3. Find the specific latent heat of fusion and use it to identify the material which:
   a) Requires 360000 J to melt 2 kg.
   b) Requires 297000 J to melt 4.5 kg.
   c) Requires 42.5 MJ to melt 125 kg.

d) Requires 82.5 kJ to melt 75 g.
e) Requires 0.11 GJ to melt 1 tonne.
f) Requires 22.5 J to melt 0.9 g.
g) Requires 27500J to melt 25g.
h) Requires 66J to melt 1g.
i) Requires 10MJ to melt 400kg.
j) Requires 1.375MJ to melt 1250g

4a) Calculate the specific latent heat of vaporisation and use it to identify the substance which requires 13680000 J of energy to evaporate 24kg.
b) Calculate the specific latent heat of vaporisation and use it to identify the substance which requires 5220000 J of energy to evaporate 6kg.
c) Calculate the specific latent heat of vaporisation and use it to identify the substance which requires 36800000 J of energy to evaporate 16kg.
d) Calculate the specific latent heat of vaporisation and use it to identify the substance which requires 7200000 J of energy to evaporate 18kg.
e) Calculate the specific latent heat of vaporisation and use it to identify the substance which requires 29900000 J of energy to evaporate 13kg.
f) Calculate the specific latent heat of vaporisation and use it to identify the substance which requires 400000 J of energy to evaporate 1kg.
g) Calculate the specific latent heat of vaporisation and use it to identify the substance which requires 6020000 J of energy to evaporate 7kg.
h) Calculate the specific latent heat of vaporisation and use it to identify the substance which requires 9570000 J of energy to evaporate 11kg.
i) Calculate the specific latent heat of vaporisation and use it to identify the substance which requires 3440000 J of energy to evaporate 4kg.
j) Calculate the specific latent heat of vaporisation and use it to identify the substance which requires 18400000 J of energy to evaporate 8kg.

1.
   a) 132000J
   b) 17.6MJ
   c) 20KJ
   d) 153KJ
   e) 748KJ
   f) 4MJ
   g) 370.5KJ
   h) 287.5KJ
   i) 791.2KJ
   j) 1792J

2.
   a) 2.9kg
   b) 1.65kg
   c) 0.4kg
   d) 0.05kg
   e) 681.8kg
   f) 9kg
   g) 2.5kg
   h) 4kg
   i) 0.033kg
   j) 3.70kg

3.
   a) Carbon Dioxide
   b) Aluminium
   c) Water
   d) Gold
   e) Ethanol
   f) Lead
   g) Gold
   h) Aluminium
   i) Lead
   j) Ethanol

4.
   a) Carbon Dioxide
   b) Lead
   c) Water
   d) Aluminium
   e) Water
   f) Aluminium
   g) Ethanol
   h) Lead
   i) Ethanol
   j) Water

4.3.3.1 Particle motion in gases

1. Draw a diagram of the particles in a gas.
2. Describe the motion of the particles in a gas.
3. What is meant by "Kinetic Energy"?
4. If the temperature of the gas in increased, what happens to the kinetic energy of the particles in the gas?
5. If the temperature of the gas in decreased, what happens to the kinetic energy of the particles in the gas?
6. Explain how the movement of the particles in the gas causes pressure on the walls of the container that the gas is in.
7. What happens to the pressure of the gas if the temperature is increased. Explain your answer.
8. What happens to the pressure of the gas if the temperature is decreased. Explain your answer.

4.3.3.1 Particle motion in gases Answers

1. Suitable Diagram – randomly, widely spaced particles
2. Fast in all directions.
3. The movement energy of the particles
4. Increases
5. Decreases
6. As the particles move, they collide with the walls of the container. This collision causes a change in the momentum of the particles which results in a force on the walls of the container.
7. Pressure increases. Kinetic energy increases. Frequency and speed of collisions with the wall increase therefore force acting on the wall increases. Therefore pressure increases.
8. Pressure decreases. Kinetic energy decreases. Frequency and speed of collisions with the wall decrease therefore force acting on the wall decreases. Therefore pressure decreases.

$$\text{pressure} \times \text{volume} = \text{constant}$$
$$p\,V = constant$$

(Students should be able to recall and apply this equation.)

1. How can the volume of a gas be increased without increasing the amount of gas?
2. How can the volume of a gas be decreased without increasing the amount of gas?
3. Explain why an increase in the volume of a fixed mass of a gas leads to a reduced pressure. (hint: **particles**)
4. Explain why increasing the pressure of a fixed mass of gas will decrease the volume.
5. Increasing the pressure on a fixed mass of gas increases the force acting on the walls of the container. Explain this observation in terms of the particles of the gas.
6. A gas occupies 4 m^3 when the pressure is 8 Pa. What volume will it occupy at 32 Pa?
7. A gas occupies 4 m^3 when the pressure is 8 Pa. What does the pressure have to be to make the volume 12 m^3?
8. A gas occupies 64 m^3 when the pressure is 3 Pa. What volume will it occupy at 24 Pa?
9. A gas occupies 16 m^3 when the pressure is 5 Pa. What does the pressure have to be to make the volume 2 m^3?
10. A gas occupies 24 m^3 when the pressure is 1.5 Pa. What volume will it occupy at 6 Pa?
11. A gas occupies 24 m^3 when the pressure is 8 Pa. What does the pressure have to be to make the volume 1 m^3?
12. A gas occupies 1.5 m^3 when the pressure is 32 kPa. What volume will it occupy at 24 kPa?
13. A gas occupies 180 m^3 when the pressure is 16 kPa. What does the pressure have to be to make the volume 2 m^3?
14. A gas occupies 520 cm^3 when the pressure is 100 kPa. What volume will it occupy at 25 kPa?
15. A gas occupies 3600 cm^3 when the pressure is 800 Pa. What does the pressure have to be to make the volume 12 m^3?

4.3.3.2 Pressure in gases (physics only) (PV = k) Answers

1. Increase the temperature/Decrease Pressure
2. Decrease the temperature/Increase Pressure
3. Number of particles remains the same but they take up more space so there are fewer collisions with the side of the container therefore less pressure.
4. Increasing pressure pushes the particles closer together causing them to take up less space therefore volume decreases.
5. The same amount of particles are in a smaller space therefore they collide with the walls more frequently increasing the pressure.
6. $1 m^3$
7. 2.7 Pa
8. $8 m^3$
9. 40 Pa
10. $6 m^3$
11. 192 Pa
12. $2 m^3$
13. 1440 kPa
14. $2080 cm^3$
15. 0.24 Pa

4.3.3.3 Increasing the pressure of a gas (physics only) (HT only)

1. What is the definition of Work?
2. The diagram shows a syringe full of air with the hole blocked with glue. Draw the particles of the gas.

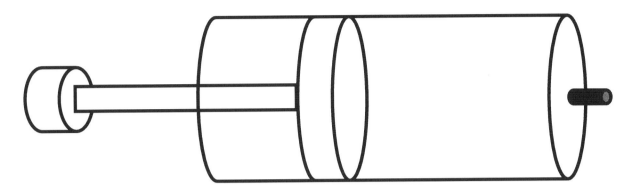

3. The piston is now moved to a new position in the diagram below. Draw the new positions of the gas particles.

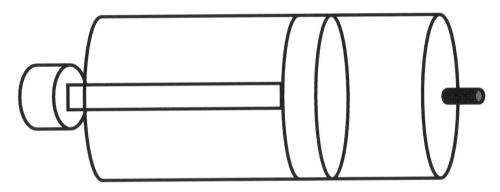

4. Describe the motion of the gas particles.
5. What has happened to the energy of the particles?
6. Explain why the gas in the syringe will now be at a higher temperature.
7. Gemma is pumping up the tyres on her bicycle with a hand pump. As she pumps she notices that the pump becomes hot. Explain this observation.

4.3.3.3 Increasing the pressure of a gas (physics only) (HT only) Answers

1. Work is the transfer of energy by a force.
2. Suitable diagram – particles spread out.
3. Suitable diagram – same number of particles, closer together.
4. The particles are now closer together, colliding more with each other and the sides. They are moving randomly and in all directions, quickly.
5. Energy increased.
6. Particles colliding more with each other and sides.
7. The particles are colliding more with the sides. The increased collisions cause a rise in temperature.

4.4.1.1 and 2 The Structure of an Atom, Mass number, Atomic Number and Isotopes

1. What is the approximate radius of an atom in metres.
2. What are the three components of an atom? Describe each component in terms of charge, mass and location within the atom.
3. What fraction of an atom is the nucleus?
   a) In terms of mass
   b) In terms of size
4. How are the electrons arranged around the nucleus?
5. What is meant by the word "absorption"?
6. What is meant by the word "emission"?
7. What will be seen when an electron moves from a higher energy level to a lower energy level?
8. What will be seen when an electron moves from a lower energy level to a higher energy level?
9. An atom is always neutral. Explain why this is true in terms of sub-atomic particles.
10. What is the same about all atoms of the same element?
11. How is the Mass Number of an element found?
12. This is the symbol for Potassium $^{39}_{19}K$
    a) What is its Mass Number?
    b) What is its Atomic Number?
13. This is the symbol for Aluminium. $^{27}_{13}Al$
    a) How many protons does Aluminium have?
    b) How many electrons does Aluminium have?
    c) How many neutrons does Aluminium have?
14. This is the symbol for Iron. $^{56}_{28}Fe$
    a) How many protons does Iron have?
    b) How many electrons does Iron have?
    c) How many neutrons does Iron have?
15. Define the term "Isotope".
16. Hydrogen has three Isotopes: ^1H, ^2H and ^3H. Describe the differences between them and explain why they are all Hydrogen.
17. What is an "Ion"?
18. This is the symbol for Nitrogen: $^{14}_{7}N$. What ion would be formed if a Nitrogen atom:
    a) Lost 1 electron
    b) Lost 2 electrons
    c) Lost 3 electrons
    d) Gained 1 electron
    e) Gained 2 electrons
    f) Gained 3 electrons

1. 1×10^{-10} m
2. Proton, +1, 1 AMU, Nucleus.
   Neutron, 0, 1 AMU, Nucleus.
   Electron, -1, Negligible/1/2000, Orbits/Shells/Orbitals, etc
3.
    a) Almost all
    b) 1/10000
4. In discrete orbits or shells.
5. Energy is absorbed in the form of electromagnetic radiation.
6. Energy is emitted in the form of electromagnetic radiation.
7. Energy will be emitted in the form of electromagnetic radiation. So light of a specific wavelength/frequency will be seen.
8. Energy will be absorbed in the form of electromagnetic radiation. So light of a specific wavelength/frequency will be absorbed and a black line will be seen in the spectrum.
9. The number of protons = the number of electrons
10. The number of protons.
11. Adding the number of protons and electrons
12.
    a) 39
    b) 19
13.
    a) 13
    b) 13
    c) 14
14.
    a) 28
    b) 28
    c) 28
15. Atoms of the same element with different numbers of neutrons.
16. They have 0, 1 and 2 neutrons respectively. All have 1 proton.
17. An atom which has gained or lost electrons.
18.
    a) N^+
    b) N^{2+}
    c) N^{3+}
    d) N^-
    e) N^{2-}
    f) N^{3-}

4.4.1.3 The Development of the Model of the Atom (common content with chemistry)

1. What does the word "atom" mean?
2. From which language does it come?
3. Who first proposed the idea of atoms?
4. Which was the first sub-atomic particle to be discovered?
5. Who discovered it?
6. The discovery of this particle lead to a theory about the atom. What was the model called?
7. Describe the atomic model named in question 6.
8. Ernest Rutherford proposed an experiment carried out by Geiger and Marsden which changed the idea of the structure of the atom. What was this experiment called?
9. Describe the set-up of Rutherford's experiment.
10. What were the observations from Rutherford's experiment?
11. What was the new structure of the atom proposed as a result of this experiment?
12. Niels Bohr adapted this new theoretical structure for the atom. Describe the Bohr atom.
13. What particles were discovered in the nucleus?
14. How was the proton discovered?
15. Who discovered the neutron?
16. The Development of the Model of the Atom shows how new experimental evidence may lead to a scientific model being changed or replaced. List and explain the new evidence that developed the model of the atom and why scientists changed their theories.

4.4.1.3 The Development of the Model of the Atom (common content with chemistry) Answers

1. The smallest part of an element that can exist
2. From Greek (atomos) meaning indivisible.
3. Democritus
4. Electron
5. J.J. Thomson
6. The Plum Pudding Model
7. Negative electrons spread throughout a positive atom
8. Alpha Scattering Experiment
9. Thin gold foil in a vacuum. Alpha particle "fired" at it from a lead lined container with a small hole in it to send a narrow beam at the gold foil. Alpha particle detector placed at different angles around the gold foil.
10. Most particles go straight through. Some deflected through small angles, some large, some reflected straight back.
11. Small positive nucleus with most of the mass, surrounded by orbits of negative electrons.
12. The electrons are in discrete shells which can only contain a certain number of electrons.
13. Protons and Neutrons
14. By subdividing the charge of a nucleus and seeing that the number of charged particles is equal to the number of electrons
15. James Chadwick
16. Appropriate timeline of development of the atom with evidence and scientists and dates.

4.4.2.1 Radioactive Decay and Nuclear Radiation

1. What is the structure of an alpha particle?
2. What is it the same as?
3. What is the penetrating power of an alpha particle?
4. What is the range in air of an alpha particle?
5. What is the ionising power of an alpha particle?
6. Describe a use of alpha particles and explain why alpha particles are suitable for this purpose.
7. What is the structure of a beta particle?
8. How is a beta particle formed in the nucleus?
9. What is the penetrating power of a beta particle?
10. What is the range in air of a beta particle?
11. What is the ionising power of a beta particle?
12. Describe a use of beta particles and explain why beta particles are suitable for this purpose.
13. What is the structure of a gamma ray?
14. What is the penetrating power of a gamma ray?
15. What is the range in air of a gamma ray?
16. What is the ionising power of a gamma ray?
17. Describe a use of gamma rays and explain why gamma rays are suitable for this purpose.
18. One other particle can be emitted from the nucleus. What is it?
19. Alpha particles, beta particles, gamma rays and neutrons can all be emitted from the nucleus. Why can their emission not be predicted?
20. Define the term "activity".
21. What are the units of activity?
22. How can activity be measured?

4.4.2.1 Radioactive Decay and Nuclear Radiation Answers

1. 2 protons and 2 neutrons
2. A helium nucleus
3. Very low
4. About 5cm
5. High
6. Smoke detector. Low penetrating power, etc
7. Fast moving electron
8. Neutron splits into a proton and an electron
9. Moderate
10. About 2m
11. Moderate
12. Thickness testing. Moderate penetrating power, etc
13. High frequency wave
14. Very high
15. Very high
16. Very low
17. Sterilisation. High Energy, etc
18. Neutron
19. Totally random
20. Number of disintegrations per second
21. Becquerel (Bq) or Counts per second (cps)
22. Geiger Counter, etc

4.4.2.2 Nuclear Equations

1. What symbol is used in nuclear equations for:
   a) an alpha particle?
   b) a beta particle?
2. Copy and complete the following nuclear equations:

   a) $^{40}_{19}K \rightarrow ^{40}_{20}Ar +$

   b) $^{239}_{94}Pu \rightarrow ^{235}_{92}U +$

   c) $^{89}_{38}Sr \rightarrow ^{89}_{39}Y +$

   d) $^{241}_{95}Am \rightarrow ^{237}_{93}Np +$

   e) $^{234}_{90}Th \rightarrow ^{234}_{91}Pa +$

   f) $^{237}_{93}Np \rightarrow ^{233}_{91}Pa +$

   g) $^{14}_{6}C \rightarrow ^{14}_{7}N +$

   h) $^{219}_{86}Rn \rightarrow ^{215}_{84}Po +$

   i) $^{211}_{83}Bi \rightarrow ^{207}_{81}Tl +$

   j) $^{32}_{15}P \rightarrow ^{32}_{16}S +$

3. Lead (Mass Number 209, Atomic Number 82) decays by beta emission to form Bismuth. What are the mass and atomic numbers for the Bismuth atoms formed from this decay?
4. Polonium (Mass Number 204, Atomic Number 84) decays by alpha emission to form Lead. What are the mass and atomic numbers for the Lead atoms formed from this decay?
5. Nickel (Mass Number 63, Atomic Number 28) decays by beta emission to form Copper. What are the mass and atomic numbers for the Copper atoms formed from this decay?
6. Lawrencium (Mass Number 256, Atomic Number 103) decays by alpha emission to form Mendelevium. What are the mass and atomic numbers for the Mendelevium atoms formed from this decay?
7. Iodine (Mass Number 131, Atomic Number 53) decays by beta emission to form Xenon. What are the mass and atomic numbers for the Xenon atoms formed from this decay?
8. Radium (Mass Number 220, Atomic Number 88) decays by alpha emission to form Radon. What are the mass and atomic numbers for the Radon atoms formed from this decay?
9. Gold (Mass Number 201, Atomic Number 79) decays to form Mercury (Mass Number 201, Atomic Number 80). Write an equation to show whether this is Alpha or Beta decay.
10. Protactinium (Mass Number 231, Atomic Number 91) decays to form Actinium (Mass Number 227, Atomic Number 89). Write an equation to show whether this is Alpha or Beta decay.
11. Gold (Mass Number 185, Atomic Number 79) decays to form Iridium (Mass

Number 181, Atomic Number 77). Write an equation to show whether this is Alpha or Beta decay.

12. Iron (Mass Number 52, Atomic Number 26) decays to form Cobalt (Mass Number 52, Atomic Number 27). Write an equation to show whether this is Alpha or Beta decay.

13. The emission of what causes no change to the mass or charge of the nucleus of an atom?

4.4.2.2 Nuclear Equations Answers

1.
   a) $^{4}_{2}He$
   b) $^{0}_{-1}e$ (accept β for e)

2.
   a) Beta
   b) Alpha
   c) Beta
   d) Alpha
   e) Beta
   f) Alpha
   g) Beta
   h) Alpha
   i) Alpha
   j) Beta
3. 209, 83
4. 200, 82
5. 63, 29
6. 252, 101
7. 131, 54
8. 218,86
9. Beta
10. Alpha
11. Alpha
12. Beta
13. Gamma Wave

4.4.2.3 Half-lives and the Random Nature of Radioactive Decay

1. Define the term "Half-Life".
2. Explain why radioactive decay cannot be predicted.
3. Plot a graph of the following radioactive decay data:

Time (s)	0	5	10	15	20	25	30	35	40	45	50	55	60	65	70
Count Rate	800	670	600	560	400	340	280	240	200	170	140	120	100	85	71

    a) Determine the half-life of the radioactive isotope.
    b) How many complete half-lives are covered on this graph?

4. Plot a graph of the following radioactive decay data:

Time (s)	0	10	20	30	40	50	60	70	80	90	100	110	120	130	140
Count Rate	1200	985	810	660	545	445	365	300	245	200	165	135	110	91	75

    a) Determine the half-life of the radioactive isotope.
    b) How many complete half-lives are covered on this graph?

5. Plot a graph of the following radioactive decay data:

Time (mins)	0	1	2	3	4	5	6	7	8	9	10	11	12	13	14
Count Rate	1000	880	780	685	604	530	470	415	365	320	285	250	220	195	170

    a) Determine the half-life of the radioactive isotope.
    b) How many complete half-lives are covered on this graph?

6. Plot a graph of the following radioactive decay data:

Time (hours)	0	2	4	6	8	10	12	14	16	18	20	22	24	26	28
Count Rate	1500	945	595	375	235	150	95	60	37	25	15	10	6	4	2

    a) Determine the half-life of the radioactive isotope.
    b) How many complete half-lives are covered on this graph?

7. 1024 g of a radioactive substance has a half-life of 8 minutes.
   a) How many grams remain after 8 minutes?
   b) How many grams remain after 24 minutes?
   c) How many grams remain after 40 minutes?
   d) How many grams remain after 56 minutes?
   e) After how many minutes will there be 256 g remaining?
   f) After how many minutes will there be 64 g remaining?
   g) After how many minutes will there be 8 g remaining?
   h) After how many minutes will there be 0.5 g remaining?

8. 32.768 kg of a radioactive substance has a half-life of 10 days.
   a) How many grams /kilogrammes remain after 10 days?
   b) How many grams /kilogrammes remain after 40 days?
   c) How many grams /kilogrammes remain after 100 days?
   d) How many grams /kilogrammes remain after 150 days?
   e) After how many days will there be 256 g remaining?
   f) After how many days will there be 64 g remaining?
   g) After how many days will there be 8 g remaining?
   h) After how many days will there be 0.5 g remaining?

4.4.2.3 Half-lives and the Random Nature of Radioactive Decay Answers

1. The half-life of a radioactive isotope is the time it takes for the number of nuclei of the isotope in a sample to halve, or the time it takes for the count rate (or activity) from a sample containing the isotope to fall to half its initial level.
2. It is a Random Process
3. Suitable Graph
   a) 20s
   b) 3
4. Suitable Graph
   a) 35s
   b) 4
5. Suitable Graph
   a) 5.5 minutes
   b) 2
6. Suitable Graph
   a) 3 hours
   b) 9
7.
   a) 512g
   b) 128g
   c) 32g
   d) 8g
   e) 16 minutes
   f) 32 minutes
   g) 56 minutes
   h) 88 minutes
8.
   a) 16.384 kg
   b) 2.048 kg
   c) 0.032 kg = 32g
   d) 1g
   e) 70 days
   f) 90 days
   g) 120 days
   h) 160 days

4.4.2.4 Radioactive contamination

1. Define the term "Radioactive Contamination".
2. What is "Decontamination"?
3. Define the term "Irradiation".
4. Which of the following are examples of Radioactive Contamination and which are examples of Irradiation. Some may be both.
   a) The effects on the environment from the Chernobyl accident.
   b) Exposing strawberries to gamma rays.
   c) A spill of radioactive material on the floor of a laboratory.
   d) Sterilising surgical equipment.
   e) Rags or cloths used to wipe up a spillage.
   f) Cancer therapies.
   g) Fallout from a nuclear bomb test.
   h) Water leaking from a damaged nuclear power station (e.g. Fukushima after the tsunami in Japan)
   i) Treating plastics with beta particles to improve cross-linking.
   j) Exposing mail to gamma rays to kill dangerous bacteria.
5. Make a list of the dangers of Radioactive Contamination.
6. Make a list of the dangers of Irradiation.
7. During Irradiation or Decontamination people need to be protected. Outline the different ways those involved can be protected from sources of radioactivity.
8. After the Fukushima nuclear disaster in 2011, the Japanese government increased the safe working levels of radioactivity for workers from 100 millisieverts to 250 millisieverts. Some scientists agreed with this change and some did not. Explain whether you would agree with the change or not and what would need to happen for a scientist to change their mind on an important issue like this.

4.4.2.4 Radioactive Contamination Answers

1. Radioactive contamination is the unwanted presence of materials containing radioactive atoms on other materials.
2. The process of removing contamination
3. Irradiation is the process of exposing an object to nuclear radiation. The irradiated object does not become radioactive
4.
    a) Contamination and Irradiation
    b) Irradiation
    c) Contamination
    d) Irradiation
    e) Contamination
    f) Irradiation
    g) Both
    h) Contamination
    i) Irradiation
    j) Irradiation
5. Radioactive sources may go to places where they are not wanted, the contamination may be difficult to remove and therefore expose humans and other organisms to dangerous radiation which could be ingested, etc
6. If the level is too high, can lead to cell/dna damage. If the level is too low, it may not kill all of the pathogens it is targeting.
7. Pro change – safe level is set very low already and an increase in safe level does not mean a commensurate rise in risk.
    Anti-change – just changing the defined risk level does not change the exposure for people.
    Scientists would need to see evidence in favour of and against the change. The problem is that this would need time and during that time people would be exposed and possibly damaged/die.

4.4.3.1 Background Radiation (physics only)

1. What is background radiation?
2. Explain how the level of background radiation in a classroom could be measured.
3. What are the units of radiation?
4. What is an approximate value for background radiation in your school?
5. Why does background radiation vary:
   a) from day to day in the same location.
   b) from location to location around the world.
6. Make a list of natural sources of background radiation.
7. Make a list of man-made sources of background radiation.
8. Explain why:
   a) A worker at a nuclear power plant may be exposed to higher than normal levels of background radiation.
   b) A pilot or astronaut may be exposed to higher than normal levels of background radiation.
   c) A radiographer may be exposed to higher than normal levels of background radiation.
   d) Someone who lives in parts of Cornwall, West Wales or the Scottish Highlands.
9. Before carrying out an experiment to determine the level of radioactivity in a sample, a scientist determines the background radiation in her laboratory.
   a) Explain why she does this.
   b) What does she do with her result once she has it?
10. What are the units of radioactive dose?

4.4.3.1 Background Radiation (physics only) Answers

1. The radiation that is around us all of the time from natural and man made sources.
2. Using a GM Tube or other suitable counter. Measure at different times of day and year and locations within the room to get a mean result.
3. Becquerel, Counts per Second (cps)
4. Anywhere between 1 and 5 Bq
5.
   a) Radioactivity is random. An area may randomly be exposed to an outside source slightly above the rest for a brief period. Eg Levels of cosmic radiation may be slightly higher that day.
   b) Some locations have naturally higher levels than others. Eg higher altitude = higher cosmic radiation, Some locations have higher natural radon gas, etc.
6. Cosmic, food, Radon gas, etc
7. Medical uses, Nuclear power, bomb tests, etc
8.
   a) They are working close to a source of radioactivity. Inadequate shielding or unavoidable workplace exposure could account for this.
   b) Layers of the Earth's atmosphere absorb and reflect harmful radiation. The higher one goes (eg pilot or astronaut) the less protection therefore higher exposure
   c) Radiographers deal with radioactive sources. Inadequate shielding or unavoidable workplace exposure could account for this.
   d) Naturally high levels of Radon gas is reported in some of parts of these regions. This can elevate exposure levels.
9.
   a) This reading will affect her results. It will be a zero error.
   b) She subtracts the mean background reading from all of her results.
10. Sieverts / Millisieverts

1. Define the term "half-life".
2. Explain how radioactive isotopes can be used to monitor the condition of organs inside the body.
3. Explain how radioactive isotopes can be used to control or destroy unwanted tissue inside the body.
4. Why is the use of radioactive isotopes preferable to traditional surgery?
5. The half-life of the isotopes used in these procedures is usually about 4 hours. Explain why this is a suitable half-life for the procedure.
6. What is a potential risk to the patient of using radioactive isotopes in these procedures?
7. Explain ways in which these risks to the patient are minimised.
8. What is a potential risk to the medical staff of using radioactive isotopes in these procedures?
9. Explain ways in which these risks to the medical staff are minimised.
10. Marie Curie carried out most of her pioneering work in the early part of the 20th Century, approximately 100 years ago. The notebooks that she used are still too contaminated with radioactivity to be safely read by anyone without protection. They will not be safe to read for several thousand years as they are contaminated with isotopes of Radium and Polonium
    a) What does this tell us of the half-lives of the isotopes of these two elements?
    b) How do you think the books are currently stored?
    c) What are the dangers of handling the notebooks?
    d) How do you think the notebooks became contaminated?
    e) What does this tell us of Marie Curie's working techniques? Explain why you think she was not more careful.
    f) Of what do you think Marie Curie died?
    g) How could Marie Curie have protected herself?
    h) Explain why these isotopes are not used in nuclear medicine.

1. The half-life of a radioactive isotope is the time it takes for the number of nuclei of the isotope in a sample to halve, or the time it takes for the count rate (or activity) from a sample containing the isotope to fall to half its initial level.
2. A radioactive source is entered into the body (ingested, injected, etc). The isotope goes to the targeted organ. The progress of the isotope is monitored by counters (gamma cameras) outside of the body.
3. Radioactivity affects DNA (ionisation). This ionisation can destroy the cells DNA or can control it to affect growth.
4. Less invasive. Still being developed – massive potential. More targeted. Etc
5. The time is long enough to carry out the procedure but short enough to ensure that there is a negligible amount left in the body after about 1 day.
6. The radiation can affect healthy organs and organ systems.
7. Short half life, low doses, targeted treatments, shielding, etc
8. Their organs can be affected in the same way as the healthy organs of a patient.
9. Shielding, low doses, monitoring, etc
10.
    a) Very long
    b) Lead lined containers, etc
    c) Exposure to ionising radiation, damage to cells and organs, etc
    d) Spills, mishandling of sources, carelessness, etc
    e) She did not fully accept the risks/dangers associated with the sources with which she was dealing
    f) Radiation poisoning/Radiation induced cancer/disease (this is disputed but it is a fair assumption for the students to make from the data given)
    g) Lead aprons, glove boxes, shielding, etc
    h) The half life is too long and the activity is too high.

1. What is the definition of Nuclear Fission?
2. Give examples of 2 elements that undergo nuclear fission.
3. Usually, a nucleus must be hit by what in order to undergo fission?
4. Draw a labelled diagram which shows how a nucleus of Uranium undergoes fission.
5. How many neutrons are usually formed in a fission reaction?
6. What happens to these neutrons?
7. Describe a chain reaction.
8. Draw a diagram of a chain reaction.
9. In a nuclear reactor, how is the chain reaction controlled?
10. What happens if a chain reaction is not controlled?
11. Give one use for an uncontrolled nuclear reaction.
12. Define Nuclear Fusion.
13. Describe Nuclear Fusion.
14. Where does Nuclear Fusion occur?
15. Nuclear Fusion gives out a lot of energy. Where does this energy come from?

4.4.4.1 Nuclear Fission and 4.4.4.2 Nuclear Fusion (physics only) Answers

1. Nuclear fission is the splitting of a large and unstable nucleus.
2. Uranium, Plutonium, Thorium, etc
3. A neutron
4. Suitable diagram
5. 2 or 3
6. They collide with other nuclei
7. An unstable nucleus splits into two emitting 3 neutrons. Those 3 neutrons travel on and split 3 further nuclei. This causes 9 neutrons to be emitted which will split 9 further nuclei and so on.
8. Suitable diagram
9. Control rods (eg Boron) absorb the extra neutrons
10. A nuclear explosion eg bomb or accident (eg Chernobyl)
11. Nuclear (atomic) bombs
12. Nuclear fusion is the joining of two light nuclei to form a heavier nucleus.
13. In a star, four hydrogen nuclei are forced together by gravity to become a helium nucleus.
14. In a star
15. The mass of the original nuclei (from $E=mc^2$)

4.5.1.1 Scalar and Vector Quantities

1. What is the difference between a Scalar quantity and a Vector quantity?
2. Make a list of some scalar quantities.
3. Make a list of some vector quantities.
4. Use a piece of string and a rule to find the distance travelled in each of the following journeys. Use a rule to find the displacement for each of the journeys.

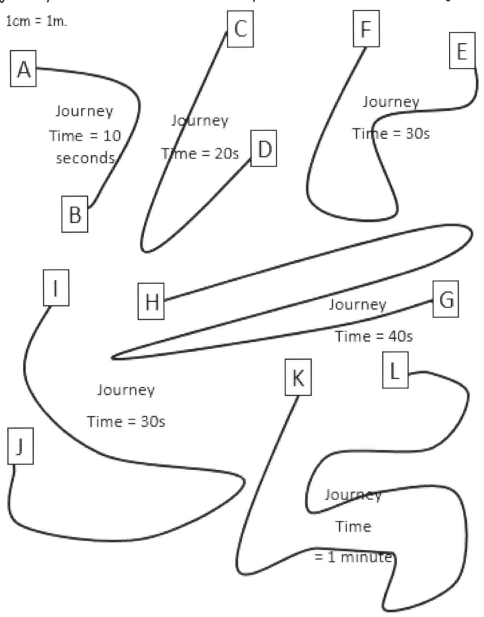

5. For each of the journeys above, calculate the speed.
6. For each of the journeys above, calculate the velocity.
7. A BMX cyclist completes 1 circuit of a 1km at a constant speed.
   a) If she completes 1 circuit in 50 seconds, calculate her speed.
   b) Explain why her velocity is not constant.
8. The moon orbits the Earth at a constant speed but not a constant velocity. Explain this statement.

4.5.1.1 Scalar and Vector Quantities Answers

1. Vector has direction, Scalar does not
2. Distance, Speed, Time
3. Acceleration, Velocity, Momentum, Displacement

Answers for q4 are approximate and the approximations will carry over into q5 and q6.

4. A-B   7m   4m
   C-D   10m   3m
   E-F   14m   3m
   G-H   28m   8m
   I-J   18m   4m
   K-L   30m   2.5m

5. A-B   0.7m/s
   C-D   0.5m/s
   E-F   0.47m/s
   G-H   0.7m/s
   I-J   0.6m/s
   K-L   0.5m/s

6. A-B   0.4m/s
   C-D   0.15m/s
   E-F   0.1m/s
   G-H   0.2m/s
   I-J   0.13m/s
   K-L   0.042m/s

7.
   a) 1000/50 = 20m/s
   b) Changing Direction

8. The moon completes an orbit in the same amount of time each month so covers the same distance in the same time so the speed in constant. However the velocity changes since the direction changes.

4.5.1.3 Gravity (mg)

weight = mass x gravitational field strength

$$W = m \, g$$

(Students should be able to recall and apply this equation.)

Body	Gravitational Field Strength, g [N/kg]
Sun	274
Mercury	3.6
Venus	8.9
Moon	1.6
Mars	3.8
Jupiter	26
Saturn	11
Uranus	10.7
Neptune	14
Pluto	0.4
Earth	9.8

1. Find the Weight of a mass of:
   a) 3kg on Earth
   b) 12 kg on Earth
   c) 1 kg on the Moon
   d) 5 kg on Saturn
   e) 0.65 kg on Jupiter
   f) 128 kg on Uranus
   g) 83 kg on Pluto
   h) 360 g on the Sun
   i) 45 g on Venus
   j) 9 g on Mars
2. What is the mass of a body which weighs:
   a) 98 N on Earth
   b) 49 N on Earth
   c) 27.4 N on the Sun
   d) 98 N on Neptune
   e) 54 N on Mercury
   f) 120 N on Pluto
   g) 0.52 N on Jupiter
   h) 2470 N on Mars
   i) 133.75 kN on Uranus
   j) 95.7 MN on Saturn

3. On which body in the solar system does:
   a) A mass of 4 kg weigh 39.2 N
   b) A mass of 4 kg weigh 14.4 N
   c) A mass of 12 kg weigh 4.8 N
   d) A mass of 15 kg weigh 160.5 N
   e) A mass of 175 kg weigh 665 N
   f) A mass of 280 kg weigh 3920 N
   g) A mass of 400 g weigh 3.56 N
   h) A mass of 8 tonnes weigh 12800 N
   i) A mass of 1 g weigh 0.274 N
   j) A mass of 0.86 kg weigh 9.46 N

1.
   a) 29.4 N
   b) 117.6 N
   c) 1.6 N
   d) 55 N
   e) 16.9N
   f) 1369.6 N
   g) 33.2 N
   h) 98.64 N
   i) 0.4 N
   j) 0.0342 N
2.
   a) 10 kg
   b) 5 kg
   c) 0.1 kg
   d) 7 kg
   e) 15 kg
   f) 300 kg
   g) 0.02 kg = 20g
   h) 650 kg
   i) 12500 kg
   j) 8700000 kg = 870 tonnes
3.
   a) Earth
   b) Mercury
   c) Pluto
   d) Uranus
   e) Mars
   f) Neptune
   g) Venus
   h) The Moon
   i) The Sun
   j) Saturn

4.5.1.2 Contact and non-contact forces and 4.5.1.4 Resultant forces and 4.5.6.2.1 Newton's First Law

1. Is Force a scalar or vector quantity? Explain your answer with 2 examples.
2. What is the definition of a "Contact Force"?
3. Give 4 examples of Contact Forces.
4. What is the definition of a "Non-Contact Force"?
5. Give 3 examples of Non-Contact Forces.
6. Define Resultant Force.
7. What is Newton's First Law?
8. Draw a diagram of book on a table. Use arrows to show the direction of the forces acting on it and use the size of the arrows to show the size of the forces.
9. Draw a diagram of a hanging basket of flowers on a hook. Use arrows to show the direction of the forces acting on it and use the size of the arrows to show the size of the forces.
10. Draw a diagram of a falling parachutist. Use arrows to show the direction of the forces acting on her and use the size of the arrows to show the size of the forces.
11. Draw a diagram of a skier going downhill. Use arrows to show the direction of the forces acting on her and use the size of the arrows to show the size of the forces.
12. If the resultant force on an object is zero there are two possibilities. What are they?
13. What happens if the resultant force on an object is not zero?
14. Determine the resultant force on the following cars.

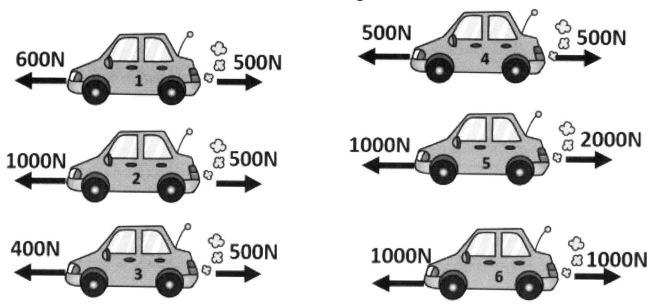

15. For each of the cars in q14, say whether it will accelerate, decelerate or maintain a steady speed.

16. Determine the magnitude and direction for the resultant force in each of these diagrams (Hint – redraw all onto graph or squared paper and measure the resultant and angle)

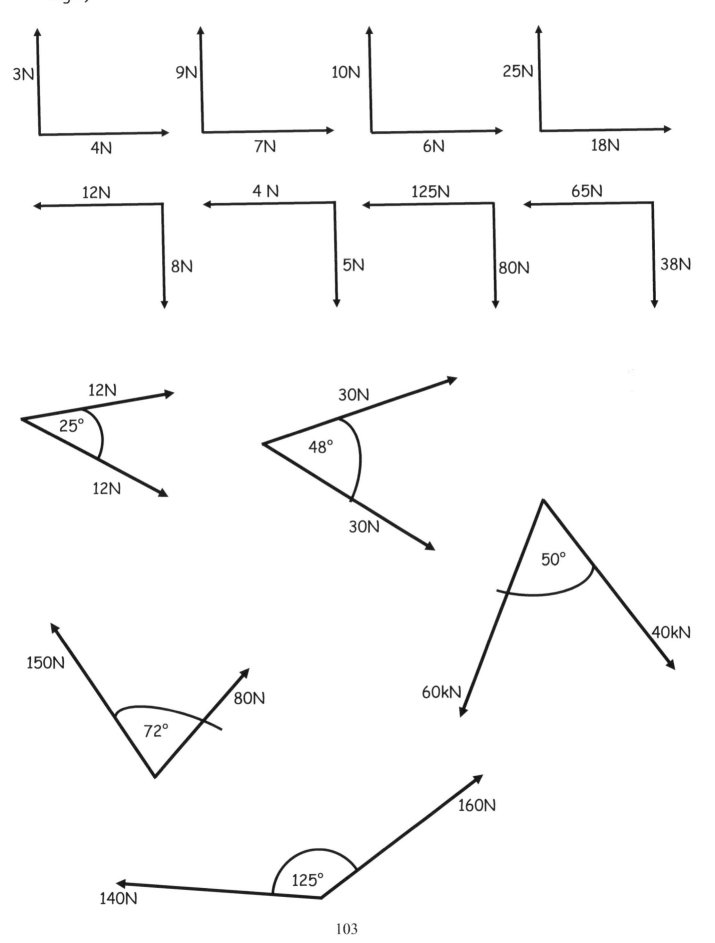

4.5.1.2 Contact and non-contact forces and 4.5.1.4 Resultant forces and 4.5.6.2.1 Newton's First Law Answers

1. Vector. Gravity downwards, Reaction upwards, etc
2. A force which needs to touch a body in order to have an effect
3. Reaction, Tension, Air Resistance, Friction, etc
4. A force which has an effect at a distance
5. Electrostatics, Gravity, Magnetism
6. When two or more forces act on an object, the **resultant force** can be found by adding up the individual forces
7. An object at rest stays at rest and an object in motion stays in motion with the same speed and in the same direction unless acted upon by an unbalanced force
8. Suitable Diagram showing same sized arrows up and down
9. Suitable Diagram showing same sized arrows up and down
10. Suitable Diagram. An explanation of the size of the arrows depending on constant speed, acceleration or deceleration
11. Suitable Diagram showing force down the hill (accept this as gravity) and friction upwards. An explanation for the size of the arrows regarding slowing down, speeding up or constant speed is necessary.
12. Constant Speed or Stationary
13. Accelerate or Decelerate or Change Direction or Change Shape
14.
    1. 100N left
    2. 500N left
    3. 100N right
    4. 0N
    5. 1000N right
    6. 0N
15.
    1. Accelerate
    2. Accelerate
    3. Decelerate
    4. Stationary/Constant Speed
    5. Decelerate
    6. Stationary/Constant Speed
16. The answers given are calculated using pythagoras and the sine and cosine rules. Students are only required to complete using scale drawing so accept some variation from "true" values.
    1. 5 N at 36.87° above horizontal
    2. 12 N at 51.13° above horizontal
    3. 11.66 N at 59.04° above horizontal
    4. 30.81 N at 54.25° above horizontal
    5. 14.42 N at 33.69° below horizontal
    6. 6.40 N at 51.34° below horizontal

7. 148.41 N at 32.62° below horizontal
8. 75.29 N at 30.31° below horizontal
9. 23.43 N at 12.5° to either of the forces
10. 54.81 N at 24° to either of the forces
11. 190.57 N at 48.5° to the 80 N force
12. 91k N at 30.3° to the 40 kN force
13. 139.66 N at 69.6° to the 140 N force

4.5.2 Work Done and Energy Transfer

Work Done = force x distance (moved along the line of action of the force)

$$W = F \, s$$

(Students should be able to recall and apply this equation.)

1. Calculate the Work Done when:
   a) A Force of 4 N moves through a distance of 3 m.
      How much energy is transferred?
   b) A Force of 8 N moves through a distance of 6 m.
      How much energy is transferred?
   c) A Force of 12.5 N moves through a distance of 2.4 m.
      How much energy is transferred?
   d) A Force of 320 N moves through a distance of 180 m.
      How much energy is transferred?
   e) A Force of 900 N moves through a distance of 3 km.
      How much energy is transferred?
   f) A Force of 450 mN moves through a distance of 55 m.
      How much energy is transferred?
   g) A Force of 250 N moves through a distance of 75 cm.
      How much energy is transferred?
   h) A Force of 6.2 kN moves through a distance of 800 cm.
      How much energy is transferred?
   i) A Force of 0.765 MN moves through a distance of 0.95 km.
      How much energy is transferred?
   j) A Force of 8.75 GN moves through a distance of 220 mm.
      How much energy is transferred?

2. Find the Force when:
   a) 35 J of work is done by a force moving a distance of 7 m.
   b) 5300 J of work is done by a force moving a distance of 55 m.
   c) 280 J of work is done by a force moving a distance of 40 m.
   d) 8.4 kJ of work is done by a force moving a distance of 3.5 km.
   e) 640 kJ of work is done by a force moving a distance of 75 m.
   f) 20 J of energy is transferred when a force moves a distance of 5 m.
   g) 1.8 J of energy is transferred when a force moves a distance of 0.6 m.
   h) 880 J of energy is transferred when a force moves a distance of 110 cm.
   i) 0.56 MJ of energy is transferred when a force moves a distance of 12 km.
   j) 1400 mJ of energy is transferred when a force moves a distance of 25 cm.

3. Determine the Distance Moved:
   a) When 48 J of work is done on a force of 12 N.
   b) When 52 J of work is done on a force of 4 N.
   c) When 320 J of work is done on a force of 24 N.
   d) When 630 kJ of work is done on a force of 900 N.
   e) When 7.5 MJ of work is done on a force of 1500 N.

f) When 85 J of energy is transferred by a force of 1.7 N.

g) When 6.5 J of energy is transferred by a force of 0.13 N.

h) When 780 mJ of energy is transferred by a force of 0.65 N.

i) When 99 kJ of energy is transferred by a force of 3 kN.

j) When 5.8 MJ of energy is transferred by a force of 0.29 kN.

4.5.2 Work Done and Energy Transfer Answers

1. In all answers the work done = energy transferred.
   a) 12 J
   b) 48 J
   c) 30 J
   d) 57.6 kJ
   e) 2.7 MJ
   f) 24.75 J
   g) 187.5 J
   h) 49.6 kJ
   i) 726.75 MJ
   j) 1.925 GJ

2.
   a) 5 N
   b) 96.36 N
   c) 7 N
   d) 2.4 N
   e) 800 N
   f) 4 N
   g) 3 N
   h) 800 N
   i) 46.7 N
   j) 5.6 N

3.
   a) 4 m
   b) 13 m
   c) 13.3 m
   d) 700 m
   e) 5 km
   f) 50 m
   g) 50 m
   h) 1.2 m
   i) 33 m
   j) 20 km

4.5.3 Forces and Elasticity (F = ke)

Force = spring constant x extension
$$F = k\,e$$
(Students should be able to recall and apply this equation.)
Give all answers to 2 significant figures.

1a) Find the force needed to extend a spring by 4m when the spring constant is 52.3N/m
b) Find the force needed to extend a cable by 1m when the spring constant is 10.1N/m
c) Find the force needed to extend a spring by 2.1m when the spring constant is 6.6N/m
d) Find the force needed to extend a cable by 1.6m when the spring constant is 43.4N/m
e) Find the force needed to extend a spring by 9.7m when the spring constant is 81N/m
f) Find the force needed to extend a spring by 10m when the spring constant is 64.1N/m
g) Find the force needed to extend a cable by 4.5mm when the spring constant is 18N/m
h) Find the force needed to extend a spring by 5.3mm when the spring constant is 71.3N/m
i) Find the force needed to extend a cable by 6.1cm when the spring constant is 41.6N/m
j) Find the force needed to extend a spring by 8.4mm when the spring constant is 70.9N/m

2a) What is the extension of a spring with spring constant 85.9N/m when a force of 0.2N acts on it?
b) What is the extension of a spring with spring constant 28.8N/m when a force of 6N acts on it?
c) What is the extension of a cable with spring constant 7.9N/m when a force of 0.4N acts on it?
d) What is the extension of a spring with spring constant 31N/m when a force of 6.6N acts on it?
e) What is the extension of a spring with spring constant 77.3N/m when a force of 7.4N acts on it?
f) What is the extension of a spring with spring constant 48.3N/m when a force of 6.9N acts on it?
g) What is the extension of a cable with spring constant 47.7N/m when a force of 5.4kN acts on it?
h) What is the extension of a cable with spring constant 6.8N/m when a force of 1.6GN acts on it?
i) What is the extension of a cable with spring constant 54N/m when a force of 2.3kN acts on it?
j) What is the extension of a cable with spring constant 48.9N/m when a force of 3.1MN acts on it?

3a) Find the spring constant of a spring which extends by 3.1m when a force of 34.2N acts on it.
b) Find the spring constant of a spring which extends by 10m when a force of 511.4N acts on it.
c) Find the spring constant of a spring which extends by 8.1m when a force of 624.8N acts on it.
d) Find the spring constant of a spring which extends by 5.2m when a force of 204.3N acts on it.
e) Find the spring constant of a spring which extends by 0.3m when a force of 552.9N acts on it.
f) Find the spring constant of a spring which extends by 3.7m when a force of 704.7N acts on it.
g) Find the spring constant of a spring which extends by 7.8mm when a force of 498kN acts on it.
h) Find the spring constant of a spring which extends by 7.7km when a force of 950.7kN acts on it.
i) Find the spring constant of a spring which extends by 4.3mm when a force of 947.9MN acts on it.
j) Find the spring constant of a spring which extends by 4.5cm when a force of 199.6GN acts on it.

4a) Determine the force acting on a length of wire with spring constant of 9000 N/m which extends by 5.5 m
b) Determine the spring constant of a piece of chewing gum which extends by 4.7 m with a force acting on it of 7000 N
c) Calculate the spring constant of a piece of chewing gum which extends by 4.1 m with a force acting on it of 50 N

d) Find the spring constant of a section of rail track which extends by 1.1 m with a force acting on it of 800 N

e) Determine the spring constant of a section of rail track which extends by 7.6 m with a force acting on it of 5 N

f) Determine the spring constant of a piece of chewing gum which extends by 1.4 m with a force acting on it of 80 N

g) Find the force acting on a piece of chewing gum with spring constant of 60 N/m which extends by 3.3 m

h) Determine the force acting on a section of rail track with spring constant of 800 N/m which extends by 9.4 m

i) Find the spring constant of a section of rail track which extends by 2.2 m with a force acting on it of 7 N

j) Find the extension of a piece of chewing gum with a force acting on it of 6000 N and a spring constant of 1 N/m

4.5.3 Forces and Elasticity Answers

1a) 210N
b) 10N
c) 14N
d) 69N
e) 790N
f) 640N
g) 0.081N
h) 0.38N
i) 2.5N
j) 0.6N

2a) 0.0023m
b) 0.21m
c) 0.051m
d) 0.21m
e) 0.096m
f) 0.14m
g) 110m
h) 240000000m
i) 43m
j) 63000m

3a) 11N/m
b) 51N/m
c) 77N/m
d) 39N/m
e) 1800N/m
f) 190N/m
g) 64000000N/m
h) 120N/m
i) 220000000000N/m
j) 4400000000000N/m

4a) 50000 N
b) 1500 N/m
c) 12 N/m
d) 730 N/m
e) 0.66 N/m
f) 57 N/m
g) 200 N
h) 7500 N
i) 3.2 N/m
j) 6000 m

4.5.4 Moments, Levers and Gears (physics only)

Moment of a force = force x distance
$$M = F \, d$$
(Students should be able to recall and apply this equation.)
Give all answers to 2 significant figures.

1. Define a moment.
2. Give 3 examples or using a force to cause a rotation.
3. Without increasing the force, how can the moment of a force be increased?
4. A mechanic is trying to remove a wheel nut from a car but it is too tight for her. How can she adapt her tool to help her remove the wheel nut? Draw a suitable diagram.
5. Explain the following:
   a) Garden shears have long handles.
   b) A long metal pole can be used to move a heavy rock.
   c) Door handles are on the opposite edge of the door to the hinge.
   d) It is better to hold cycle handle bars at the end.
   e) Pliers have long handles.
   f) How gears can be used to transmit the rotational effect of a force.

6a) Determine the moment of a force of 100 N acting at a distance of 0.6 m from the pivot.
b) Determine the moment of a force of 8000 N acting at a distance of 8.6 m from the pivot.
c) Determine the moment of a force of 2000 N acting at a distance of 1.4 m from the pivot.
d) Determine the moment of a force of 8000 N acting at a distance of 4.8 m from the pivot.
e) Determine the moment of a force of 1000 N acting at a distance of 2.8 m from the pivot.
f) Determine the moment of a force of 2000 N acting at a distance of 1 m from the pivot.
g) Determine the moment of a force of 1.3MN acting at a distance of 3.6mm from the pivot.
h) Determine the moment of a force of 5.8GN acting at a distance of 8.8mm from the pivot.
i) Determine the moment of a force of 3.1kN acting at a distance of 6.4mm from the pivot.
j) Determine the moment of a force of 4.3kN acting at a distance of 7.5mm from the pivot.

7a) What force is needed to give a moment of 3000Nm acting at a distance of 0.2 m from the pivot.
b) What force is needed to give a moment of 70Nm acting at a distance of 7.4 m from the pivot.
c) What force is needed to give a moment of 900Nm acting at a distance of 3.1 m from the pivot.

d) What force is needed to give a moment of 50Nm acting at a distance of 6.6 m from the pivot.

e) What force is needed to give a moment of 7000Nm acting at a distance of 1 m from the pivot.

f) What force is needed to give a moment of 9000Nm acting at a distance of 5.3 m from the pivot.

g) What force is needed to give a moment of 1000Nm acting at a distance of 2.9cm from the pivot.

h) What force is needed to give a moment of 1000Nm acting at a distance of 2.6cm from the pivot.

i) What force is needed to give a moment of 5000Nm acting at a distance of 7.3cm from the pivot.

j) What force is needed to give a moment of 500Nm acting at a distance of 7.8mm from the pivot.

8a) What is the distance from the pivot that a force of 800N has to act to give a moment of 800Nm.

b) What is the distance from the pivot that a force of 900N has to act to give a moment of 4000Nm.

c) What is the distance from the pivot that a force of 8000N has to act to give a moment of 50Nm.

d) What is the distance from the pivot that a force of 40N has to act to give a moment of 200Nm.

e) What is the distance from the pivot that a force of 300N has to act to give a moment of 500Nm.

f) What is the distance from the pivot that a force of 20N has to act to give a moment of 4000Nm.

g) What is the distance from the pivot that a force of 1.9MN has to act to give a moment of 200000Nm.

h) What is the distance from the pivot that a force of 8.5MN has to act to give a moment of 600000Nm.

i) What is the distance from the pivot that a force of 7.5kN has to act to give a moment of 800000Nm.

j) What is the distance from the pivot that a force of 9.1GN has to act to give a moment of 500000Nm.

9a) What is the distance from the pivot that a force of 7000N has to act to balance a force of 60N acting at a distance of 6.4 m on the opposite side of the pivot?

b) What is the distance from the pivot that a force of 60N has to act to balance a force of 60N acting at a distance of 8.3 m on the opposite side of the pivot?

c) What is the distance from the pivot that a force of 300N has to act to balance a force of 70N acting at a distance of 4.4 m on the opposite side of the pivot?

d) What is the distance from the pivot that a force of 20N has to act to balance a force of 5000N acting at a distance of 9.2 m on the opposite side of the pivot?

e) What is the distance from the pivot that a force of 1000N has to act to balance a force of 8000N acting at a distance of 5.3 m on the opposite side of the pivot?
f) What is the distance from the pivot that a force of 900N has to act to balance a force of 7000N acting at a distance of 9.8 m on the opposite side of the pivot?
g) What is the distance from the pivot that a force of 1000N has to act to balance a force of 6000N acting at a distance of 4.1 m on the opposite side of the pivot?
h) What is the distance from the pivot that a force of 700N has to act to balance a force of 3000N acting at a distance of 9.3 m on the opposite side of the pivot?
i) What is the distance from the pivot that a force of 700N has to act to balance a force of 5000N acting at a distance of 3 m on the opposite side of the pivot?
j) What is the distance from the pivot that a force of 8000N has to act to balance a force of 4000N acting at a distance of 7.1 m on the opposite side of the pivot?

10a) What force is needed to act at a distance of 3.3 m on the opposite side of the pivot to a force of 50N acting at a distance of 6 m?
b) What force is needed to act at a distance of 5.5 m on the opposite side of the pivot to a force of 50N acting at a distance of 6.1 m?
c) What force is needed to act at a distance of 5.3 m on the opposite side of the pivot to a force of 6000N acting at a distance of 7.7 m?
d) What force is needed to act at a distance of 2.9 m on the opposite side of the pivot to a force of 1000N acting at a distance of 2.1 m?
e) What force is needed to act at a distance of 1.9 m on the opposite side of the pivot to a force of 70N acting at a distance of 8.1 m?
f) What force is needed to act at a distance of 9.6 m on the opposite side of the pivot to a force of 7000N acting at a distance of 8.8 m?
g) What force is needed to act at a distance of 7.1 m on the opposite side of the pivot to a force of 70N acting at a distance of 2.3 m?
h) What force is needed to act at a distance of 9.4 m on the opposite side of the pivot to a force of 9000N acting at a distance of 3 m?
i) What force is needed to act at a distance of 3.1 m on the opposite side of the pivot to a force of 500N acting at a distance of 4.2 m?
j) What force is needed to act at a distance of 8.9 m on the opposite side of the pivot to a force of 1000N acting at a distance of 7.2 m?

4.5.4 Moments, Levers and Gears (physics only) Answers

1. Moment = Force x Perpendicular Distance from pivot
2. Spanner, scissors, doors, etc
3. Increase the distance of the force from the pivot
4. Lengthen the handle of the spanner + Suitable Diagram
5.
   a) To increase force at the blades
   b) Force at the end of the pole furthest from the pivot only needs to be small to produce a big force at the other end to move the rock.
   c) The distance from the hinge is large so that a small force is needed to produce a bigger moment.
   d) Holding handles at the end means that a smaller force is needed to turned the wheels
   e) A smaller force is needed to squeeze the handles
   f) The number of teeth on one gear relative to the number on another will increase or decrease the speed of the rotation. The number of gears will determine the direction of the rotation.

6a) 60Nm
b) 69000Nm
c) 2800Nm
d) 38000Nm
e) 2800Nm
f) 2000Nm
g) 4700Nm
h) 51000000Nm
i) 20Nm
j) 32Nm

8a) 1m
b) 4.4m
c) 0.0063m
d) 5m
e) 1.7m
f) 200m
g) 0.11m
h) 0.071m
i) 110m
j) 0.000055m

9a) 0.055m
b) 8.3m
c) 1m
d) 2300m
e) 42m
f) 76m
g) 25m
h) 40m
i) 21m
j) 3.6m

7a) 15000N
b) 9.5N
c) 290N
d) 7.6N
e) 7000N
f) 1700N
g) 34000N
h) 38000N

i) 68000N
j) 64000N

10a) 91N
b) 55N
c) 8700N
d) 720N
e) 300N
f) 6400N
g) 23N
h) 2900N
i) 680N
j) 810N

4.5.5.1.1 Pressure in a fluid 1 (physics only)

$$Pressure = \frac{force}{area}$$

$$P = \frac{F}{A}$$

(Students should be able to recall and apply this equation.)

1. Calculate the Pressure when:
   a) A Force of 12 N acts on an area of 4 m².
   b) A Force of 360 N acts on an area of 18 m².
   c) A Force of 480 N acts on an area of 6 m².
   d) A Force of 5.6 N acts on an area of 0.7 m².
   e) A Force of 0.38 N acts on an area of 1.9 m².
   f) A Force of 7.2 kN acts on an area of 160 m².
   g) A Force of 650 MN acts on an area of 1300 m².
   h) A Force of 9.24 GN acts on an area of 25 000 m².
   i) A Force of 5.50 mN acts on an area of 1.1 mm².
   j) A Force of 280 mN acts on an area of 4 cm².

2. Determine the Force when:
   a) An Area of 8 m² experiences a Pressure of 6 Pa.
   b) An Area of 45 m² experiences a Pressure of 12 Pa.
   c) An Area of 9.1 m² experiences a Pressure of 7.2 Pa.
   d) An Area of 260 m² experiences a Pressure of 520 Pa.
   e) An Area of 0.9 m² experiences a Pressure of 85 Pa.
   f) An Area of 700 m² experiences a Pressure of 0.11 kPa.
   g) An Area of 400 mm² experiences a Pressure of 250 Pa.
   h) An Area of 12 mm² experiences a Pressure of 30 MPa.
   i) An Area of 0.5 km² experiences a Pressure of 4.2 kPa.
   j) An Area of 6200 mm² experiences a Pressure of 520 mPa.

3. Find the Area when:
   a) A Force of 25 N causes a Pressure of 5 Pa.
   b) A Force of 72 N causes a Pressure of 16 Pa.
   c) A Force of 8.4 N causes a Pressure of 2.1 Pa.
   d) A Force of 0.48 N causes a Pressure of 4.0 Pa.
   e) A Force of 640 N causes a Pressure of 20 Pa.
   f) A Force of 9.5 kN causes a Pressure of 38 Pa.
   g) A Force of 120 kN causes a Pressure of 80 kPa.
   h) A Force of 56 MN causes a Pressure of 0.7 MPa.
   i) A Force of 320 MN causes a Pressure of 600 kPa.
   j) A Force of 4200 mN causes a Pressure of 0.6 Pa.

4.5.5.1.1 Pressure in a fluid 1 (physics only) Answers

1.
   a) 3 Pa
   b) 20 Pa
   c) 80 Pa
   d) 8 Pa
   e) 0.2 Pa
   f) 45 Pa
   g) 500 kPa
   h) 369.9 kPa
   i) 5 kPa
   j) 700 Pa

2.
   a) 48 N
   b) 540 N
   c) 65.52 N
   d) 135.2 kN
   e) 76.5 N
   f) 77 kN
   g) 0.1 N
   h) 360 N
   i) 2.1 GN
   j) 3.224 mN

3.
   a) 5 m²
   b) 4.5 m²
   c) 4 m²
   d) 0.12 m²
   e) 32 m²
   f) 250 m²
   g) 1.5 m²
   h) 80 m²
   i) 5333 m²
   j) 7 m²

4.5.5.1.2 Pressure in a fluid 2 (physics only) (HT only)

Pressure = height of the column x density of the liquid x gravitational field strength
$$P = h \rho g$$
(Students should be able to apply this equation which is given on the *Physics Equation Sheet*.)
Give all answers to 2 significant figures.

1a) What is the pressure exerted by a 28m high column of liquid with a density of 0.8 kgm^{-3}?
b) What is the pressure exerted by a 1.2m high column of liquid with a density of 2.5 kgm^{-3}?
c) What is the pressure exerted by a 69.3m high column of liquid with a density of 4.8 kgm^{-3}?
d) What is the pressure exerted by a 12m high column of liquid with a density of 4.7 kgm^{-3}?
e) What is the pressure exerted by a 29.7m high column of liquid with a density of 4.7 kgm^{-3}?
f) What is the pressure exerted by a 79.4m high column of liquid with a density of 2.7 kgm^{-3}?
g) What is the pressure exerted by a 16.4cm high column of liquid with a density of 4.4 kgm^{-3}?
h) What is the pressure exerted by a 97.9mm high column of liquid with a density of 1.2 kgm^{-3}?
i) What is the pressure exerted by a 15.5cm high column of liquid with a density of 4.9 kgm^{-3}?
j) What is the pressure exerted by a 58km high column of liquid with a density of 2.3 kgm^{-3}?

2a) A pressure of 937 Pa is exerted by a column of liquid of height 46m. What is its density?
b) A pressure of 1234 Pa is exerted by a column of liquid of height 69.2m. What is its density?
c) A pressure of 1486 Pa is exerted by a column of liquid of height 92.8m. What is its density?
d) A pressure of 532 Pa is exerted by a column of liquid of height 59.1m. What is its density?
e) A pressure of 394 Pa is exerted by a column of liquid of height 8.2m. What is its density?
f) A pressure of 2255 Pa is exerted by a column of liquid of height 61m. What is its density?
g) A pressure of 1610 Pa is exerted by a column of liquid of height 43.7mm. What is its density?
h) A pressure of 1832 Pa is exerted by a column of liquid of height 67.7km. What is its density?
i) A pressure of 1874 Pa is exerted by a column of liquid of height 17.4mm. What is its density?
j) A pressure of 726 Pa is exerted by a column of liquid of height 3km. What is its density?

3a) A pressure of 1988 Pa is exerted by a column of liquid of density 4.5 kgm^{-3}. What is the height of the column of liquid?
b) A pressure of 1950 Pa is exerted by a column of liquid of density 1.4 kgm^{-3}. What is the height of the column of liquid?
c) A pressure of 330 Pa is exerted by a column of liquid of density 1.2 kgm^{-3}. What is the height of the column of liquid?
d) A pressure of 685 Pa is exerted by a column of liquid of density 1.4 kgm^{-3}. What is the height of the column of liquid?
e) A pressure of 2430 Pa is exerted by a column of liquid of density 4.2 kgm^{-3}. What is the height of the column of liquid?
f) A pressure of 2326 Pa is exerted by a column of liquid of density 4.9 kgm^{-3}. What is the height of the column of liquid?
g) A pressure of 1241 Pa is exerted by a column of liquid of density 3.2 kgm^{-3}. What is the height of the column of liquid?
h) A pressure of 1560 Pa is exerted by a column of liquid of density 3.5 kgm^{-3}. What is the height of the column of liquid?
i) A pressure of 527 Pa is exerted by a column of liquid of density 4.1 kgm^{-3}. What is the height of the column of liquid?
j) A pressure of 1044 Pa is exerted by a column of liquid of density 3.3 kgm^{-3}. What is the height of the column of liquid?

4.5.5.1.2 Pressure in a Fluid 2 (physics only) (HT only) Answers

1a) 220 Pa
b) 29 Pa
c) 3300 Pa
d) 550 Pa
e) 1400 Pa
f) 2100 Pa
g) 7.1 Pa
h) 1.2 Pa
i) 7.4 Pa
j) 1300000 Pa

2a) 2.1 kgm^{-3}
b) 1.8 kgm^{-3}
c) 1.6 kgm^{-3}
d) 0.92 kgm^{-3}
e) 4.9 kgm^{-3}
f) 3.8 kgm^{-3}
g) 3800 kgm^{-3}
h) 0.0028 kgm^{-3}
i) 11000 kgm^{-3}
j) 0.025 kgm^{-3}

3a) 45 m
b) 140 m
c) 28 m
d) 50 m
e) 59 m
f) 48 m
g) 40 m
h) 45 m
i) 13 m
j) 32 m

4.5.5.2 Atmospheric Pressure (physics only)

1. What is the Earth's atmosphere?
2. Name 4 gases in the Earth's atmosphere.
3. Explain the changes in the Earth's atmosphere as the distance from the Earth increases.
4. Explain pressure in terms of gas particles.
5. The pressure at the summit of Mount Everest is about 34000 Pascals. The pressure at sea level is about 100000 Pascals. Explain this difference.
6. Mountaineers can find cooking difficult when climbing Everest as the boiling point of water on the mountain is about 71°C. Explain why this is the case. (Hint: Use data from the previous question). What can the mountaineers do to solve this problem?

4.5.5.2 Atmospheric Pressure (physics only) Answers

1. A thin layer of a mixture of gases around the earth.
2. Nitrogen, Oxygen, Carbon Dioxide, Argon, etc
3. The atmosphere becomes less dense the further away from the Earth.
4. Pressure is caused by gas particles colliding with the sides of a container or other items.
5. Above the sea, the height of the atmosphere is greater than that above the summit of Mount Everest so the pressure is less.
6. There is a greater pressure pushing the particles back into the vessel at sea level than at the summit therefore more energy is needed to boil it at sea level.

4.5.6.1.2 Speed and 4.5.6.1.3 Velocity

Distance Travelled = speed x time

$$s = v\,t$$

(Students should be able to recall and apply this equation.)

1. Calculate the Distance Travelled by an object moving at:
   a) 8 m/s for 3 s.
   b) 10 m/s for 9 s.
   c) 15 m/s for 45 s.
   d) 20 m/s for 18 s.
   e) 25 m/s for 60 s.
   f) 40 mm/s for 18 s.
   g) 24 m/s for 2 minutes.
   h) 75 mm/s for 20 minutes.
   i) 2 km/s for 3 minutes.
   j) 15 m/s for 1.5 hours.

2. Find the Speed when an object moves:
   a) 30 m in 6 s.
   b) 80 m in 20 s.
   c) 750 m in 25 s.
   d) 900 m in 150 s.
   e) 8400 m in 3 minutes.
   f) 5.2 km in 10 minutes.
   g) 4.2 km in 3.5 minutes.
   h) 250 km in 2 hours.
   i) 500 mm in 10 ms.
   j) 180 mm in 6 s.

3. Determine the Time Taken to travel: *(In these questions, convert the answers to the most suitable units of time)*
   a) 75 m at 5 m/s.
   b) 144 m at 12 m/s.
   c) 840 m at 30 m/s.
   d) 1500 m at 25 m/s.
   e) 20 km at 15 m/s.
   f) 500 km at 12.5 m/s.
   g) 16 m at 4 cm/s.
   h) 55 cm at 8 mm/s.
   i) 180 mm at 2 cm/s.
   j) 6.35 m at 105 mm/s.

4a) Find the speed of a car with a distance travelled of 3.5 m in a time of 4.5 s

b) Find the time of travel of a bus with a speed of 4.2 m/s in a distance of 1.7 m

c) Determine the distance travelled of a train with a speed of 5.9 m/s in a time of 4.3 s

d) Calculate the time of travel of a train with a speed of 8.9 m/s in a distance of 9.1 m

e) Determine the distance travelled of a bus with a speed of 9.9 m/s in a time of 9.4 s

f) Determine the time of travel of a train with a speed of 5.6 m/s in a distance of 6.9 m

g) Find the time of travel of a bus with a speed of 10 m/s in a distance of 1.3 m

h) Determine the speed of a car with a distance travelled of 2.4 m in a time of 9.5 s

i) Find the speed of a bus with a distance travelled of 3.6 m in a time of 4.6 s

j) Determine the time of travel of a train with a speed of 5.4 m/s in a distance of 3 m

4.5.6.1.2 Speed and 4.5.6.1.3 Velocity Answers

1.
a) 24m
b) 90m
c) 675m
d) 360m
e) 1500m
f) 720mm
g) 2880m
h) 90m
i) 360km
j) 81km

2.
a) 5m/s
b) 4m/s
c) 30m/s
d) 6m/s
e) 46.7m/s
f) 8.7m/s
g) 20m/s
h) 34.7m/s = 125km/h
i) 50m/s
j) 0.03m/s

3.
a) 15s
b) 12s
c) 28s
d) 60s = 1minute
e) 1333s = 22 minutes 13s
f) 40000s = 11 hours 6minutes 40s
g) 400s = 6minutes 40s
h) 68.75s
i) 9s
j) 60.5s

4
a) 0.78 m/s
b) 0.4 s
c) 25 m
d) 1 s
e) 93 m
f) 1.2 s
g) 0.13 s
h) 0.25 m/s
i) 0.78 m/s
j) 0.56 s

4.5.6.1.1 Distance and displacement and 4.5.6.1.4 The distance–time relationship

1. What is the difference between a scalar quantity and a vector quantity?
2. Explain the difference between distance and displacement.
3. On a distance-time graph, which quantity is plotted on:
   a) The x axis.
   b) The y axis.
4. How can a distance-time graph be used to find the speed?
5. If the distance-time graph is curved upwards, what is happening?
6. If the distance-time graph is curved downwards, what is happening?
7. If the distance-time graph is curved, how can the speed be found?
8. If the distance-time graph is a straight horizontal line, what does this show?
9. The table shows the distance a walker travels in a certain time. Plot a graph of the data.

Time (s)	0	2	4	6	8	10	12	14	16	18	20	22	24	26	28
Distance (m)	0	3	6	9	12	15	18	21	24	27	30	30	30	30	30

   a) Determine the speed of the walker in the first 20 s.
   b) What is the speed of the walker after 20 s?
   c) What is the average speed of the walker over the whole journey?
   d) Describe the journey

10. The table shows the distance a runner travels in a certain time. Plot a graph of the data.

Time (s)	0	5	10	15	20	25	30	35	40	45	50	55	60	65	70
Distance (m)	0	15	30	45	60	70	80	90	100	105	110	115	120	125	130

   a) Calculate the speed of the runner in the first 20 seconds
   b) What happens to the speed of the runner after 20 seconds?
   c) Calculate the speed of the runner between 20 and 40 seconds.
   d) What happens to the speed of the runner after 40 seconds?
   e) Calculate the speed of the runner between 40 and 70 seconds.
   f) What is the average speed of the runner over the whole journey?
   g) Describe the journey.

11. The table shows the distance a cyclist travels in a certain time. Plot a graph of the data.

Time (s)	0	10	20	30	40	50	60	70	80	90	100	110	120	130	140
Distance (m)	0	60	120	180	240	300	300	300	300	350	400	450	500	550	600

    a) Calculate the speed of the cyclist in the first 50 s.
    b) Describe the motion of the cyclist between 50 and 80 seconds?
    c) Calculate the speed of the cyclist between 80 and 140 s.
    d) What is the average speed of the cyclist over the whole journey?
    e) Describe the journey.

12. The table shows the distance a car travels in a certain time. Plot a graph of the data.

Time (s)	0	1	2	3	4	5	6	7	8	9	10	11	12	13	14
Distance (m)	0	4	8	16	32	48	64	80	96	76	66	61	58	58	58

    a) Describe the motion of the car in the first 4 seconds?
    b) Determine the speed of the car when the time is 2.5 seconds.
    c) Describe the motion of the car between 4 and 8 seconds.
    d) Determine the speed of the car between 4 and 8 s.
    e) Calculate the average speed of the car in the first 8 s.
    f) Describe the motion of the car between 8 and 14 seconds.
    g) Calculate the speed of the car at 9.5 s
    h) Describe the journey.

4.5.6.1.1 Distance and displacement and 4.5.6.1.4 The Distance-Time Relationship Answers

1. Scalar quantity has no direction, vector quantity has a direction
2. Distance is a scalar quantity, displacement is a vector quantity
3.
   a) X = time
   b) Y = distance
4. Find the gradient
5. Accelerating
6. Decelerating
7. Draw tangent and determine the gradient of the tangent
8. Stationary
9. Suitable Graph
   a) 1.5 m/s
   b) 0 m/s
   c) 1.07 m/s
   d) Walks at constant speed for 20 s then stops at 30 m from starting position and stays there for 8 s
10. Suitable Graph
    a) 3 m/s
    b) Slows down
    c) 2 m/s
    d) Slows down
    e) 1 m/s
    f) 1.86 m/s
    g) Travels at 3 m/s for the first 20s. Then slows to 2 m/s for the next 20 s. Then slows to 1 m/s for the next 30 s
11. Suitable Graph
    a) 6 m/s
    b) Stopped
    c) 5 m/s
    d) 4.29 m/s
    e) Pedals at 6 m/s for the first 50 s then stops for 30 s then pedals at 5 m/s for the next 60 s
12. Suitable Graph
    a) Increasing Speed, acceleration
    b) Tangent drawn at t=2.5s. Speed = 8 m/s (allow any reasonable answer corresponding to their gradient)
    c) Constant speed
    d) 16 m/s
    e) 96 ÷ 8 = 16 m/s
    f) Decelerating
    g) Tangent drawn at t=9.5s. Speed = 11 m/s (allow any reasonable answer corresponding to their gradient)

h) Car accelerates for first 4 seconds. Then a steady speed for the next 4 seconds. Then decelerates for 4 seconds before becoming stationary, 58 m from its starting point for the last 2 seconds.

4.5.6.1.5 Acceleration

$$\text{Acceleration} = \frac{\text{change in velocity}}{\text{time taken}}$$

$$a = \frac{\Delta v}{t} \qquad a = \frac{v-u}{t}$$

(Students should be able to recall and apply this equation.)

1a) A vehicle changes speed from 4.2 m/s to 46.7 m/s in 100 s. Calculate its acceleration.
b) A vehicle changes speed from 19.5 m/s to 38.1 m/s in 400 s. Calculate its acceleration.
c) A vehicle changes speed from 11.1 m/s to 47.4 m/s in 500 s. Calculate its acceleration.
d) A vehicle changes speed from 14.2 m/s to 40.2 m/s in 40 s. Calculate its acceleration.
e) A vehicle changes speed from 40.8 m/s to 16.2 m/s in 100 s. Calculate its deceleration.
f) A vehicle changes speed from 36.9 m/s to 3.5 m/s in 500 s. Calculate its deceleration.
g) A vehicle changes speed from 33 m/s to 17.9 m/s in 10 s. Calculate its deceleration.
h) A vehicle changes speed from 39.4 m/s to 12 m/s in 10 s. Calculate its deceleration.
i) A vehicle changes speed from 27km/h to 34.8km/h in 3 minutes. Calculate its acceleration.
j) A vehicle changes speed from 47.2km/h to 28.9km/h in 3 minutes. Calculate its deceleration.

2a) Find the change in velocity when a vehicle accelerates at 1.8 m/s² for 300 s.
b) Find the change in velocity when a vehicle accelerates at 1.7 m/s² for 50 s.
c) Find the change in velocity when a vehicle accelerates at 1.9 m/s² for 30 s.
d) Find the change in velocity when a vehicle accelerates at 2 m/s² for 500 s.
e) Find the change in velocity when a vehicle accelerates at 0.1 m/s² for 10 s.
f) Find the change in velocity when a vehicle decelerates at -0.1 m/s²for 30 s.
g) Find the change in velocity when a vehicle decelerates at -1.3 m/s² for 200 s.
h) Find the change in velocity when a vehicle decelerates at -1.3 m/s² for 500 s.
i) Find the change in velocity when a vehicle decelerates at -0.5 m/s² for 10 s.
j) Find the change in velocity when a vehicle decelerates at -1.3 m/s² for 50 s.

3a) A vehicle accelerates from rest at 0.6 m/s² for 200 s. Find its final velocity.
b) A vehicle accelerates from rest at 0.9 m/s² for 40 s. Find its final velocity.
c) A vehicle accelerates from rest at 1.9 m/s² for 50 s. Find its final velocity.
d) A vehicle accelerates from rest at 1.5 m/s²for 20 s. Find its final velocity.
e) A vehicle accelerates from rest at 1 m/s² for 30 s. Find its final velocity.
f) A vehicle accelerates from rest at 0.6 m/s² for 40 s. Find its final velocity.
g) A vehicle accelerates from rest at 1.2 m/s² for 300 s. Find its final velocity.
h) A vehicle accelerates from rest at 0.7 m/s² for 400 s. Find its final velocity.
i) A vehicle accelerates from rest at 0.3 m/s² for 5 minutes. Find its final velocity.
j) A vehicle accelerates from rest at 0.7 m/s² for 4 minutes. Find its final velocity.

4a) A vehicle decelerates to rest at -0.3 m/s² in 500 s. Find its initial velocity.
b) A vehicle decelerates to rest at -1.7 m/s² in 50 s. Find its initial velocity.

c) A vehicle d1ecelerates to rest at -1.9 m/s² in 300 s. Find its initial velocity.

d) A vehicle decelerates to rest at -0.4 m/s² in 50 s. Find its initial velocity.

e) A vehicle decelerates to rest at -0.1 m/s² in 100 s. Find its initial velocity.

f) A vehicle decelerates to rest at -0.2 m/s² in 300 s. Find its initial velocity.

g) A vehicle decelerates to rest at -1.3 m/s² in 20 s. Find its initial velocity.

h) A vehicle decelerates to rest at -1.3 m/s² in 20 s. Find its initial velocity.

i) A vehicle decelerates to rest at -1 m/s² in 3 minutes. Find its initial velocity.

j) A vehicle decelerates to rest at -1.5 m/s² in 5 minutes. Find its initial velocity.

5a) A vehicle decelerates to 11.9 m/s at -1.5 m/s² in 10 s. Find its initial velocity.

b) A vehicle decelerates to 19.7 m/s at -0.5 m/s² in 40 s. Find its initial velocity.

c) A vehicle decelerates to 13.8 m/s at -2 m/s² in 300 s. Find its initial velocity.

d) A vehicle decelerates to 23.1 m/s at -1.4 m/s² in 500 s. Find its initial velocity.

e) A vehicle decelerates to 24.5 m/s at -0.7 m/s² in 400 s. Find its initial velocity.

f) A vehicle decelerates to 24.1 m/s at -0.9 m/s² in 10 s. Find its initial velocity.

g) A vehicle decelerates to 28.8 m/s at -1.4 m/s² in 30 s. Find its initial velocity.

h) A vehicle decelerates to 21.9 m/s at -0.3 m/s² in 200 s. Find its initial velocity.

i) A vehicle decelerates to 20.8 m/s at -1.8 m/s² in 200 s. Find its initial velocity.

j) A vehicle decelerates to 10.2 m/s at -1.4 m/s² in 20 s. Find its initial velocity.

6a) A vehicle accelerates to 6.4 m/s at 1 m/s² in 400 s. Find its final velocity.

b) A vehicle accelerates to 9.8 m/s at 0.1 m/s² in 40 s. Find its final velocity.

c) A vehicle accelerates to 24.6 m/s at 1.6 m/s² in 400 s. Find its final velocity.

d) A vehicle accelerates to 8.8 m/s at 0.3 m/s² in 500 s. Find its final velocity.

e) A vehicle accelerates to 0.9 m/s at 0.4 m/s² in 30 s. Find its final velocity.

f) A vehicle accelerates to 0.4 m/s at 0.7 m/s² in 40 s. Find its final velocity.

g) A vehicle accelerates to 25.3 m/s at 1.3 m/s² in 100 s. Find its final velocity.

h) A vehicle accelerates to 28.6 m/s at 0.3 m/s² in 200 s. Find its final velocity.

i) A vehicle accelerates to 14 m/s at 0.4 m/s² in 10 s. Find its final velocity.

j) A vehicle accelerates to 25 m/s at 1.9 m/s² in 200 s. Find its final velocity.

7a) A vehicle changes speed from 4.2 m/s to 33.6 m/s at 1.9 m/s². How much time did this take?

b) A vehicle changes speed from 22.8 m/s to 30 m/s at 1.5 m/s². How much time did this take?

c) A vehicle changes speed from 6.3 m/s to 44.7 m/s at 0.2 m/s². How much time did this take?

d) A vehicle changes speed from 19 m/s to 39.1 m/s at 0.4 m/s². How much time did this take?

e) A vehicle changes speed from 7.4 m/s to 42.5 m/s at 0.8 m/s². How much time did this take?

f) A vehicle changes speed from 1.8 m/s to 37.5 m/s at 0.1 m/s². How much time did this take?

g) A vehicle changes speed from 18.3 m/s to 42.6 m/s at 0.8 m/s². How much time did this take?

h) A vehicle changes speed from 13.8 m/s to 36.7 m/s at 1.5 m/s². How much time did this take?

i) A vehicle changes speed from 13.8 m/s to 38.5 m/s at 0.8 m/s². How much time did this take?

j) A vehicle changes speed from 4.6 m/s to 39.3 m/s at 0.7 m/s². How much time did this take?

4.5.6.1.5 Acceleration Answers

1a) 0.43 m/s^2
b) 0.047 m/s^2
c) 0.073 m/s^2
d) 0.65 m/s^2
e) -0.25 m/s^2
f) -0.067 m/s^2
g) -1.5 m/s^2
h) -2.7 m/s^{2}s
i) 0.012 m/s^2
j) -0.028 m/s^2

2a) 540 m/s
b) 85 m/s
c) 57 m/s
d) 1000 m/s
e) 1 m/s
f) 3 m/s
g) 260 m/s
h) 650 m/s
i) 5 m/s
j) 65 m/s

3a) 120 m/s
b) 36 m/s
c) 95 m/s
d) 30 m/s
e) 30 m/s
f) 24 m/s
g) 360 m/s
h) 280 m/s
i) 90 m/s
j) 170 m/s

4a) 9000 m/s
b) 5100 m/s
c) 34000 m/s
d) 1200 m/s
e) 600 m/s
f) 3600 m/s
g) 1600 m/s
h) 1600 m/s
i) 180 m/s
j) 450 m/s

5a) 27 m/s
b) 40 m/s
c) 610 m/s
d) 720 m/s
e) 300 m/s
f) 33 m/s
g) 71 m/s
h) 82 m/s
i) 380 m/s
j) 38 m/s

6a) 410 m/s
b) 14 m/s
c) 660 m/s
d) 160 m/s
e) 13 m/s
f) 28 m/s
g) 160 m/s
h) 89 m/s
i) 18 m/s
j) 410 m/s

7a) 15 s
b) 4.8 s
c) 190 s
d) 50 s
e) 44 s
f) 360 s
g) 30 s
h) 15 s
i) 31 s
j) 50 s

Velocity Time Graphs

1. On a velocity-time graph, which variable goes on:
   a) the x axis
   b) the y axis
2. How can a velocity-time graph be used to determine the acceleration?
3. How does a velocity-time graph show deceleration?
4. How can a velocity-time graph be used to determine the distance travelled (displacement)?
5. The table shows how the velocity of a car changes over time. Plot a graph of the data.

Time (s)	0	1	2	3	4	5	6	7	8	9	10	11	12	13	14	15
Velocity (m/s)	0	2	4	6	8	10	12	14	16	16	16	16	12	8	4	0

   a) Describe the motion of the car between 0 and 8 s.
   b) Use the graph to determine the acceleration of the car in the first 8 s.
   c) Determine the distance travelled in the first 8 s.
   d) Describe the motion of the car between 8 and 11 seconds.
   e) Determine the distance travelled between 8 and 11s.
   f) Use the graph to determine the acceleration of the car between 11 and 15 s.
   g) Determine the distance travelled between 11 and 15 s.
   h) Determine the total distance of the journey.
   i) Describe the journey.

6. The table shows how the velocity of a train changes over time. Plot a graph of the data.

Time (s)	0	5	10	15	20	25	30	35	40	45	50	55	60	65	70
Velocity (m/s)	0	4	8	12	16	20	25	30	35	40	45	50	50	50	50

   a) Describe the motion of the train between 0 and 25 s.
   b) Use the graph to determine the acceleration of the train in the first 25 s.
   c) Determine the distance travelled in the first 25 s.
   d) Describe the motion of the train between 25 and 55 seconds.
   e) Use the graph to determine the acceleration of the train between 25 and 55 seconds.
   f) Determine the distance travelled between 25 and 55 seconds.
   g) Describe the motion of the train after 55 s.
   h) Determine the distance travelled after 55 s.
   i) Determine the total distance of the journey.
   j) Describe the journey

7. The table shows how the velocity of a racing cyclist changes over time. Plot a graph of the data.

Time (s)	0	0.5	1	1.5	2	2.5	3	3.5	4	4.5	5	5.5	6	6.5	7
Velocity (m/s)	0	2	4	6	8	10	10	10	9	8	7	6	5	5	5

a) Describe the motion of the cyclist between 0 and 2.5 s.
b) Use the graph to determine the acceleration of the cyclist in the first 2.5 s.
c) Determine the distance travelled in the first 2.5 s.
d) Describe the motion of the cyclist between 2.5 and 3.5 seconds.
e) Determine the distance travelled between 2.5 and 3.5 seconds.
f) Describe the motion of the cyclist between 3.5 and 6 seconds.
g) Use the graph to determine the acceleration of the cyclist between 3.5 and 6 seconds.
h) Determine the distance travelled between 3.5 and 6 seconds.
i) Describe the motion of the cyclist after 6 s.
j) Determine the total distance of the journey.
k) Describe the journey

8. The table shows how the velocity of a car changes over time. Plot a graph of the data.

Time (s)	0	10	20	30	40	50	60	70	80	90	100	110	120	130
Velocity (m/s)	0	3	6	9	12	15	18	21	24	24	24	16	8	0

a) Describe the motion of the car between 0 and 80 s.
b) Use the graph to determine the acceleration of the car in the first 80 s.
c) Determine the distance travelled in the first 80 s.
d) Describe the motion of the car between 80 and 100 seconds.
e) Determine the distance travelled between 80 and 100s.
f) Use the graph to determine the acceleration of the car between 100 and 130 s.
g) Determine the distance travelled between 100 and 130 s.
h) Determine the total distance of the journey.
i) Describe the journey.

9. The table shows how the velocity of a cycle changes over time. Plot a graph of the data.

Time (s)	0	1	2	3	4	5	6	7	8	9	10	11	12	13	14	15
Velocity (m/s)	0	0.5	1	2	4	8	10	11	12	12	12	6	3	2	1	0

a) Describe the motion of the car between 0 and 8 s.
b) Use the graph to determine the acceleration of the cycle at 4 s.
c) Estimate the distance travelled in the first 8 s.
d) Describe the motion of the car between 8 and 10 seconds.
e) Determine the distance travelled between 8 and 10s.
f) Describe the motion of the car between 10 and 15 s.
g) Use the graph to determine the acceleration of the cycle at 12 s.
h) Estimate the distance travelled between 10 and 15 s.
i) Determine the total distance of the journey.
j) Describe the journey.

1.
   a) Time
   b) Velocity
2. Find the gradient
3. Line of negative gradient
4. The area under the graph
5.
   a) Accelerating
   b) 2 m/s^2
   c) 64 m
   d) Constant Speed/Velocity
   e) 48 m
   f) -4m/s^2
   g) 32 m
   h) 124 m
   i) Accelerates, Constant speed, decelerates to stop
6.
   a) Accelerates from rest
   b) 0.8 m/s^2
   c) 250 m
   d) Acceleration
   e) 1 m/s^2
   f) 450 m
   g) Constant Speed/Velocity
   h) 750 m
   i) 1450 m
   j) Accelerates from rest, then accelerates at higher rate, then continues at steady speed.
7.
   a) Accelerates from rest
   b) 4 m/s^2
   c) 12.5 m
   d) Constant Speed/Velocity
   e) 10 m
   f) Decelerates
   g) 2 m/s^2
   h) 6.25 m
   i) Constant Speed/Velocity
   j) 28.75 m
   k) Accelerates from rest, stays at steady speed, decelerates, stays at new steady speed.
8.
   a) Accelerates from rest
   b) 0.3 m/s^2
   c) 960 m
   d) Constant Speed/Velocity
   e) 480 m
   f) -0.8 m/s^2

g) 360 m

h) 1800 m

i) Accelerates from rest, constant speed, decelerates to rest.

9.

a) Increasing acceleration

b) Suitable tangent drawn. Gradient calculated. 2.4 m/s^2

c) Counting squares. Approx 42 m

d) Constant Speed/Velocity

e) 24 m

f) Decreasing deceleration

g) Suitable tangent drawn. Gradient calculated. 1.7 m/s^2

h) Counting squares. Approx 17 m

i) 83 m (sum of their values)

j) Cycle increases acceleration up to 5 s then acceleration decreases to a constant speed. Cycle then decelerates to rest.

Acceleration Calculations

$$\text{(final velocity)}^2 - \text{(initial velocity)}^2 = 2 \times \text{acceleration} \times \text{distance}$$
$$v^2 - u^2 = 2\,a\,s$$

(Students should be able to apply this equation which is given on the *Physics Equation Sheet*.)
Give all answers to 2 significant figures.

1a) A vehicle changes speed from 28.6 m/s to 30.8 m/s in a distance of 30 m. Calculate its acceleration.

b) A vehicle changes speed from 9.5 m/s to 43.8 m/s in a distance of 50 m. Calculate its acceleration.

c) A vehicle changes speed from 13.9 m/s to 48 m/s in a distance of 400 m. Calculate its acceleration.

d) A vehicle changes speed from 5.9 m/s to 33.6 m/s in a distance of 5000 m. Calculate its acceleration.

e) A vehicle changes speed from 23.8 m/s to 48.1 m/s in a distance of 400 m. Calculate its acceleration.

f) A vehicle changes speed from 25.4 m/s to 30.2 m/s in a distance of 4000 m. Calculate its acceleration.

g) A vehicle changes speed from 0.4 m/s to 40.6 m/s in a distance of 100 m. Calculate its acceleration.

h) A vehicle changes speed from 16.9 m/s to 46.4 m/s in a distance of 30 m. Calculate its acceleration.

i) A vehicle changes speed from 22.8 m/s to 38.1 m/s in a distance of 20 m. Calculate its acceleration.

j) A vehicle changes speed from 6.2 m/s to 49.5 m/s in a distance of 100 m. Calculate its acceleration.

2a) A vehicle changes speed from 26.5 m/s to 37.7 m/s under an acceleration of 1 m/s^2. Find the distance travelled.

b) A vehicle changes speed from 4 m/s to 35.1 m/s under an acceleration of 0.9 m/s^2. Find the distance travelled.

c) A vehicle changes speed from 23 m/s to 35.5 m/s under an acceleration of 0.1 m/s^2. Find the distance travelled.

d) A vehicle changes speed from 6.9 m/s to 34.1 m/s under an acceleration of 0.8 m/s^2. Find the distance travelled.

e) A vehicle changes speed from 15.2 m/s to 41.8 m/s under an acceleration of 0.5 m/s^2. Find the distance travelled.

f) A vehicle changes speed from 18.8 m/s to 43.8 m/s under an acceleration of 0.6 m/s^2. Find the distance travelled.

g) A vehicle changes speed from 17.2 m/s to 33.4 m/s under an acceleration of 1.7 m/s^2. Find the distance travelled.

h) A vehicle changes speed from 13.8 m/s to 38.6 m/s under an acceleration of 1.8 m/s^2. Find the distance travelled.

i) A vehicle changes speed from 18.5 m/s to 46.5 m/s under an acceleration of 1.8 m/s^2. Find the distance travelled.

j) A vehicle changes speed from 7.5 m/s to 47.8 m/s under an acceleration of 1.6 m/s^2. Find the distance travelled.

3a) A vehicle accelerates at 1.4 m/s^2 to 23.7 m/s over a distance of 3 m. What was its initial velocity?

b) A vehicle accelerates at 0.4 m/s^2 to 49.6 m/s over a distance of 30 m. What was its initial velocity?

c) A vehicle accelerates at 0.7 m/s^2 to 46.4 m/s over a distance of 100 m. What was its initial velocity?

d) A vehicle accelerates at 0.4 m/s^2 to 42.1 m/s over a distance of 300 m. What was its initial velocity?

e) A vehicle accelerates at 0.8 m/s^2 to 45.7 m/s over a distance of 30 m. What was its initial velocity?

f) A vehicle accelerates at 0.6 m/s^2 to 44.7 m/s over a distance of 30 m. What was its initial velocity?

g) A vehicle accelerates at 1.5 m/s^2 to 34 m/s over a distance of 100 m. What was its initial velocity?

h) A vehicle accelerates at 1.3 m/s^2 to 30.3 m/s over a distance of 3 m. What was its initial velocity?

i) A vehicle accelerates at 0.9 m/s^2 to 36.3 m/s over a distance of 3 m. What was its initial velocity?

j) A vehicle accelerates at 1.5 m/s^2 to 41.2 m/s over a distance of 300 m. What was its initial velocity?

4a) A vehicle accelerates at 0.9 m/s^2 from 13.4 m/s over a distance of 700 m. Determine its final velocity.

b) A vehicle accelerates at 1.1 m/s^2 from 29.1 m/s over a distance of 30 m. Determine its final velocity.

c) A vehicle accelerates at 0.4 m/s^2 from 24.3 m/s over a distance of 300 m. Determine its final velocity.

d) A vehicle accelerates at 0.1 m/s^2 from 28.7 m/s over a distance of 4 m. Determine its final velocity.

e) A vehicle accelerates at 0.5 m/s^2 from 37.2 m/s over a distance of 60 m. Determine its final velocity.

f) A vehicle accelerates at 0.8 m/s^2 from 14.2 m/s over a distance of 2 m. Determine its final velocity.

g) A vehicle accelerates at 1.1 m/s^2 from 27.3 m/s over a distance of 80 m. Determine its final velocity.

h) A vehicle accelerates at 2 m/s^2 from 31.8 m/s over a distance of 70 m. Determine its final velocity.

i) A vehicle accelerates at 0.6 m/s^2 from 39.5 m/s over a distance of 9 m. Determine its final velocity.

j) A vehicle accelerates at 0.1 m/s^2 from 18.5 m/s over a distance of 4 m. Determine its final velocity.

Acceleration Calculations
Answers

1a) 2.2 m/s^2

b) 18 m/s^2

c) 2.6 m/s^2

d) 0.11 m/s^2

e) 2.2 m/s^2

f) 0.033 m/s^2

g) 8.2 m/s^2

h) 31 m/s^2

i) 23 m/s^2

j) 12 m/s^2

2a) 360 m

b) 680 m

c) 3700 m

d) 700 m

e) 1500 m

f) 1300 m

g) 240 m

h) 360 m

i) 510 m

j) 700 m

3a) 24 m/s

b) 49 m/s

c) 45 m/s

d) 39 m/s

e) 45 m/s

f) 44 m/s

g) 29 m/s

h) 30 m/s

i) 36 m/s

j) 28 m/s

4a) 38 m/s

b) 30 m/s

c) 29 m/s

d) 29 m/s

e) 38 m/s

f) 14 m/s

g) 30 m/s

h) 36 m/s

i) 40 m/s

j) 19 m/s

4.5.6.2.2 Newton's Second Law

Resultant Force = mass x acceleration

F = m a

(Students should be able to recall and apply this equation.)

Give all answers to 2 significant figures.

1a) A mass of 40 kg is accelerated at 8.9 m/s². Calculate the resultant force acting on it.
b) A mass of 40 kg is accelerated at 3.4 m/s². Calculate the resultant force acting on it.
c) A mass of 2000 kg is accelerated at 2.7 m/s². Calculate the resultant force acting on it.
d) A mass of 300 kg is accelerated at 4.3 m/s². Calculate the resultant force acting on it.
e) A mass of 7000 kg is accelerated at 0.6 m/s². Calculate the resultant force acting on it.
f) A mass of 400 kg is accelerated at 8 m/s². Calculate the resultant force acting on it.
g) A mass of 700mg is accelerated at 7.1 m/s². Calculate the resultant force acting on it.
h) A mass of 7g is accelerated at 8.3 m/s². Calculate the resultant force acting on it.
i) A mass of 90g is accelerated at 9 m/s². Calculate the resultant force acting on it.
j) A mass of 8mg is accelerated at 8.4 m/s². Calculate the resultant force acting on it.

2a) A mass of 300kg has a resultant force of 600N acting on it. Calculate its acceleration.
b) A mass of 6000kg has a resultant force of 9N acting on it. Calculate its acceleration.
c) A mass of 60kg has a resultant force of 200N acting on it. Calculate its acceleration.
d) A mass of 80kg has a resultant force of 7000N acting on it. Calculate its acceleration.
e) A mass of 600kg has a resultant force of 70N acting on it. Calculate its acceleration.
f) A mass of 30kg has a resultant force of 7000N acting on it. Calculate its acceleration.
g) A mass of 300kg has a resultant force of 3kN acting on it. Calculate its acceleration.
h) A mass of 10kg has a resultant force of 9GN acting on it. Calculate its acceleration.
i) A mass of 7kg has a resultant force of 3MN acting on it. Calculate its acceleration.
j) A mass of 8000kg has a resultant force of 5kN acting on it. Calculate its acceleration.

3a) What is the mass of an object which accelerates at 1.9 m/s² under a resultant force of 40N?
b) What is the mass of an object which accelerates at 1.1 m/s² under a resultant force of 6000N?
c) What is the mass of an object which accelerates at 2.3 m/s² under a resultant force of 200N?
d) What is the mass of an object which accelerates at 6.8 m/s² under a resultant force of 4N?
e) What is the mass of an object which accelerates at 8.9 m/s² under a resultant force of 50N?
f) What is the mass of an object which accelerates at 7 m/s² under a resultant force of 4000N?
g) What is the mass of an object which accelerates at 4.1 m/s² under a resultant force of 8GN?
h) What is the mass of an object which accelerates at 5 m/s² under a resultant force of 9kN?
i) What is the mass of an object which accelerates at 9.3 m/s² under a resultant force of 9GN?
j) What is the mass of an object which accelerates at 4.1 m/s² under a resultant force of 7GN?

4a) Determine the mass of a car with an acceleration of 4.3 m/s² and a force acting on it of 2 N
b) Calculate the mass of a car with an acceleration of 8.8 m/s² and a force acting on it of 8 N
c) Determine the force acting on a car with a mass of 7 kg and an acceleration of 3.1 m/s²
d) Find the force acting on a car with a mass of 800 kg and an acceleration of 1.4 m/s²
e) Find the mass of a body with an acceleration of 5.8 m/s² and a force acting on it of 7 N
f) Determine the acceleration of a body with a force acting on it of 20 N and a mass of 4000 kg

g) Find the mass of a car with an acceleration of 3.8 m/s^2 and a force acting on it of 3000 N

h) Calculate the acceleration of a car with a force acting on it of 6 N and a mass of 30 kg

i) Find the acceleration of a body with a force acting on it of 70 N and a mass of 10 kg

j) Find the acceleration of a body with a force acting on it of 100 N and a mass of 300 kg

4.5.6.2.2 Newton's Second Law Answers

1a) 360 N
b) 140 N
c) 5400 N
d) 1300 N
e) 4200 N
f) 3200 N
g) 0.005 N
h) 0.058 N
i) 0.81 N
j) 0.000067 N

4a) 0.47 kg
b) 0.91 kg
c) 22 N
d) 1100 N
e) 1.2 kg
f) 0.005 m/s^2
g) 790 kg
h) 0.2 m/s^2
i) 7 m/s^2
j) 0.33 m/s^2

2a) 2 m/s^2
b) 0.0015 m/s^2
c) 3.3 m/s^2
d) 88 m/s^2
e) 0.12 m/s^2
f) 230 m/s^2
g) 10 m/s^2
h) 900000000 m/s^2
i) 430000 m/s^2
j) 0.63 m/s^2

3a) 21 kg
b) 5500 kg
c) 87 kg
d) 0.59 kg
e) 5.6 kg
f) 570 kg
g) 2000000000 kg
h) 1800 kg
i) 970000000 kg
j) 1700000000 kg

4.5.6.2.3 Newton's Third Law

1. What is Newton's Third Law?
2. Explain how Newton's Third law applies to the following situations: (you may wish to draw a diagram to help you explain)
    a. A bag resting on a chair.
    b. A gymnast doing press ups.
    c. A boat floating on the sea.
    d. A car wheel rolling along the floor.
    e. A swimmer pushing off the side of a pool.
    f. The paddles of a canoe in the water.
    g. A football bouncing on the floor.
    h. A sprinter leaving the blocks at the start of a race.
    i. A cannon goes backwards when it is fired.
    j. A balloon as air is let out of it.
    k. A rocket taking off.
3. Can you explain why you slip when you walk on ice but not when you walk on concrete?
4. Explain why two ice skaters move in opposite directions when they push away from each other.
5. Danny is in a boat. As it comes to the bank, he stands on the edge of the boat and jumps. He misses the bank and falls in the water. Explain why.

4.5.6.2.3 Newton's Third Law Answers

1. Every action has an equal and opposite reaction
2.
   a. The bag pushes down on the chair, the chair pushes up on the bag.
   b. The gymnast pushes down on the floor, the floor pushes up on the gymnast
   c. The boat pushes down on the water, the water pushes up on the boat
   d. The wheel pushes backwards on the ground, the ground pushes forward on the wheel.
   e. The swimmer pushes back against the side of the pool, the side of the pool pushes forward against the swimmer.
   f. The paddle pushes backwards against the water, the water pushes forwards against the paddle
   g. The ball pushes downwards against the floor, the floor pushes upwards against the ball
   h. The sprinter pushes backwards against the blocks, the blocks push forwards against the sprinter
   i. The canon pushes forwards against the ball, the ball pushes backwards against the canon.
   j. The balloon pushes against the air leaving it, the air pushes against the balloon as it leaves.
   k. The rocket exerts a force of the fuel/gases leaving the rocket, the gases exert an equal and opposite force on the rocket.
3. The friction on ice is lower than the friction on concrete. When your feet push backwards on ice the forward force of the ice is very small therefore you slip. When you push back on concrete, the friction is big enough to push your feet forward.
4. The two ice skaters exert an equal and opposite force on each other.
5. As Danny tries to jump forward, his leg exerts a force on the boat, pushing it backwards so he misses the bank.

4.5.6.3.1 Stopping Distance and 4.5.6.3.3 Factors Affecting Braking Distance 1 and 4.5.6.3.4 Factors Affecting Braking Distance 2

1. What is the Thinking Distance?
2. What are the factors that affect the Thinking Distance?
3. What is the Braking Distance?
4. What are the factors that affect the Braking Distance?
5. One factor affects both Thinking and Braking Distances. What is it?
6. How is the Stopping Distance calculated?

Below is a table which gives Thinking and Braking Distances at various speeds for a car in good condition on a dry road.

7. Calculate the Stopping Distances in the following table.

Speed m/s	Thinking Distance (m)	Braking Distance (m)	Stopping Distance (m)
8	6	6	
13	9	14	
18	12	24	
23	15	38	
28	18	55	
33	21	75	

8. Plot a graph of Thinking Distance (y axis) v Speed (x axis)
9. Use your graph to estimate the Thinking Distance when the Speed is:
    a) 5 m/s
    b) 15 m/s
    c) 30 m/s
10. Use your graph to estimate the Speed when the Thinking Distance is:
    a) 5 m
    b) 10 m
    c) 20 m
11. Plot a graph of Braking Distance (y axis) v Speed (x axis)
12. Use your graph to estimate the Braking Distance when the Speed is:
    a) 15 m/s
    b) 25 m/s
    c) 35 m/s
13. Use your graph to estimate the Speed when the Braking Distance is:
    a) 10 m
    b) 40 m
    c) 60 m
14. Plot a graph of Stopping Distance (y axis) v Speed (x axis)
15. Use your graph to estimate the Stopping Distance when the Speed is:
    a) 10 m/s
    b) 20 m/s
    c) 30 m/s

16. Use your graph to estimate the Speed when the Stopping Distance is:
    a) 10 m
    b) 50 m
    c) 100 m
17. The data in the table is for a car in good condition with an alert driver on a dry road. Explain the effects on the overall stopping distance if:
    a) It was snowing
    b) The driver had been drinking alcohol
    c) The vehicle was a coach and not a car.
18. There have been studies which say that the current stopping distances published by the UK government in the Highway Code are no longer accurate. Suggest what changes have happened since the figures were first published in 1954 and explain what effects the changes will have on overall Stopping Distances.
19. When a vehicle brakes, what energy changes are taking place?
20. Explain why it takes a larger distance for a vehicle with a greater mass to stop than one with a smaller mass.
21. Explain why it takes a larger distance for a vehicle with a greater speed to stop than one with a smaller speed.
22. Which will require a greater force to stop – a vehicle with a greater mass or one with a smaller mass? Explain your answer.
23. Which will require a greater force to stop – a vehicle with a greater velocity or one with a smaller velocity? Explain your answer.
24. Large decelerations can be dangerous. Explain why.

24 a) A train of mass 10000 kg decelerates from 23 m/s to 3 m/s in 0.035 s. What is the force acting?

b) A truck of mass 80000 kg decelerates from 24 m/s to 6 m/s in 0.029 s. What is the force acting?

c) A lorry of mass 90000 kg decelerates from 15 m/s to 4 m/s in 0.097 s. What is the force acting?

d) A train of mass 50000 kg decelerates from 20 m/s to 8 m/s in 0.094 s. What is the force acting?

e) A truck of mass 80000 kg decelerates from 25 m/s to 2 m/s in 0.047 s. What is the force acting?

f) A lorry of mass 10000 kg decelerates from 13 m/s to 8 m/s in 0.089 s. What is the force acting?

g) A lorry of mass 70000 kg decelerates from 13 m/s to 8 m/s in 0.057 s. What is the force acting?

h) A train of mass 30000 kg decelerates from 12 m/s to 2 m/s in 0.029 s. What is the force acting?

i) A truck of mass 70000 kg decelerates from 18 m/s to 1 m/s in 0.1 s. What is the force acting?

j) A lorry of mass 80000 kg decelerates from 12 m/s to 1 m/s in 0.014 s. What is the force acting?

4.5.6.3.1 Stopping Distance and 4.5.6.3.3 Factors Affecting Braking Distance 1 and 4.5.6.3.4 Factors Affecting Braking Distance 2 Answers

1. The distance travelled during the driver's reaction time
2. Alcohol, distractions, drugs, etc
3. The distance travelled after the brakes have been pressed.
4. Condition of car (tyres, brakes, etc), condition of road (weather, mud, etc)
5. Speed
6. Thinking Distance + Stopping Distance
7. 12m
   23m
   36m
   53m
   73m
   96m

Questions 8 to 16 are based on the students own graphs so credit should be given if the students are ± one small square (2mm at GCSE)

8. Suitable graph
9.
   a) 4 m
   b) 10 m
   c) 19 m
10.
   a) 6 m/s
   b) 15 m/s
   c) 31.5 m/s
11. Suitable graph
12.
   a) 17 m
   b) 42 m
   c) 83 m
13.
   a) 11 m/s
   b) 24 m/s
   c) 30 m/s
14. Suitable graph
15.
   a) 16 m
   b) 41 m
   c) 80 m
16.
   a) 8 m/s
   b) 22.5 m/s
   c) 34 m/s

17.
   a) Braking distance would increase therefore stopping distance would increase
   b) Thinking distance would increase therefore stopping distance would increase
   c) Mass would increase so if it was traveling at the same speed it would have a greater momentum therefore a greater force would be needed to stop it. If the brakes were the same, the stopping distance would increase.
18. Cars are faster therefore stopping distances should be increased.
    Cars have better brakes and other technological advances therefore stopping distances should have decreased.
    Reasonable discussion around these points.
19. Kinetic to thermal (and sound)
20. Mass is higher so if it was traveling at the same speed it would have a greater momentum therefore a greater force would be needed to stop it.
21. Greater speed means greater Kinetic energy. More needs to be converted to heat so more time/distance needed to stop. Also greater momentum so more force needed to change momentum to zero.
22. Greater mass due to greater momentum. Also greater kinetic energy.
23. Greater velocity due to greater momentum. Also greater kinetic energy.

   24 a) 5700000 N
   b) 50000000 N
   c) 10000000 N
   d) 6400000 N
   e) 39000000 N
   f) 560000 N
   g) 6100000 N
   h) 10000000 N
   i) 12000000 N
   j) 63000000 N

4.5.6.3.2 Reaction time

1. Define a person's Reaction Time.
2. What is the typical reaction time for a human being?
3. Make a list of factors affect a person's reaction time.
4. Explain why reaction times are important whilst driving.
5. Which component of the Stopping Distance is affected by the Reaction Time?
6. Describe a simple experiment to determine the reaction time of a fellow student.
7. Corinne carried out a reaction time test on 10 people in her classroom. She tested each person 10 times and calculated their mean reaction time. She recorded her results in the table below.

Person	A	B	C	D	E	F	G	H	I	J
Reaction Time ms	195	263	510	426	350	841	366	288	520	472

a) What does ms stand for in the table?
b) How did Corinne convert from s to ms?
c) Why did Corinne repeat the test 10 times?
d) Corinne decided to plot her data in a chart. What type of chart should she choose? Explain your choice.
e) Plot a suitable graph to show this data.
f) Corinne used a ruler to determine her reaction times. Explain the problems associated with this method.
g) Describe another method that Corinne could have used to obtain her results and list any advantages this method may have.
h) One of the people in the test was Corinne's teacher, Mr Franklin. Give the letter of the person you think is Mr Franklin. Explain your answer.
i) One of the people in the test, Adam, is the winner of the 100 m race at the school Sports Day. Give the letter of the person you think is Adam. Explain your answer.

4.5.6.3.2 Reaction Time Answers

1. The length of time taken for a person or system to respond to a given stimulus or event.
2. 0.2 s to 0.9 s
3. Drink, drugs, tiredness, distractions, etc
4. Quicker reaction times mean shorter stopping distances
5. Thinking distance
6. Description of ruler drop experiment or use of software.
7.
    a) Milliseconds
    b) X by 1000
    c) To remove random errors/increase accuracy
    d) Bar Chart – Independent variable is a person's name/letter.
    e) Suitable chart
    f) Other person can predict when it is dropped. Is it dropped from same height? Height needs converting to time. Etc
    g) Use a computer/online program/app. More precision, repeatable, etc
    h) F - It's the biggest
    i) A – It's the smallest.

4.5.7.1 Momentum is a property of moving objects (HT only)

$$Momentum = mass \times velocity$$
$$p = m\,v$$
(Students should be able to recall and apply this equation.)

1. Determine the Momentum of an object of:
   a) mass 25 kg travelling at 2 m/s.
   b) mass 30 kg travelling at 8 m/s.
   c) mass 0.6 kg travelling at 14 m/s.
   d) mass 19 kg travelling at 0.7 m/s.
   e) mass 450 g travelling at 5 m/s.
   f) mass 30 g travelling at 40 m/s.
   g) mass 72 kg travelling at 60 cm/s.
   h) mass 0.84 kg travelling at 17 cm/s.
   i) mass 680 g travelling at 35 cm/s.
   j) mass 540 kg travelling at 55 km/h.
2. Find the Mass of an object with a:
   a) momentum of 100 kg m/s travelling at 4 m/s.
   b) momentum of 240 kg m/s travelling at 8 m/s.
   c) momentum of 150 kg m/s travelling at 3 m/s.
   d) momentum of 620 kg m/s travelling at 15.5 m/s.
   e) momentum of 0.95 kg m/s travelling at 0.5 m/s.
   f) momentum of 55 kg m/s travelling at 2.75 m/s.
   g) momentum of 360 kg m/s travelling at 18 m/s.
   h) momentum of 4800 kg m/s travelling at 72 m/s.
   i) momentum of 70 kg m/s travelling at 3.5 m/s.
   j) momentum of 850 kg m/s travelling at 21.25 m/s.
3. Calculate the Velocity of an object with a:
   a) momentum of 120 kg m/s and a mass of 60 kg.
   b) momentum of 240 kg m/s and a mass of 180 kg.
   c) momentum of 3500 kg m/s and a mass of 700 kg.
   d) momentum of 100000 kg m/s and a mass of 4000 kg.
   e) momentum of 550000 kg m/s and a mass of 11000 kg.
   f) momentum of 0.75 kg m/s and a mass of 150 g.
   g) momentum of 84 kg m/s and a mass of 700 g.
   h) momentum of 4800 g m/s and a mass of 1200 g.
   i) momentum of 690 g m/s and a mass of 130 g.
   j) momentum of 12 g m/s and a mass of 0.002 kg.

4.5.7.1 Momentum is a property of moving objects (HT only) Answers

1.
   a) 50 kg m/s
   b) 240 kg m/s
   c) 8.4 kg m/s
   d) 13.3 kg m/s
   e) 2.25 kg m/s
   f) 1.2 kg m/s
   g) 43.2 kg m/s
   h) 0.1428 kg m/s
   i) 0.238 kg m/s
   j) 8250 kg m/s

2.
   a) 25 kg
   b) 30 kg
   c) 50 kg
   d) 40 kg
   e) 109 kg
   f) 20 kg
   g) 20 kg
   h) 66.7 kg
   i) 20 kg
   j) 40 kg

3.
   a) 2 m/s
   b) 1.3 m/s
   c) 5 m/s
   d) 25 m/s
   e) 50 m/s
   f) 5 m/s
   g) 120 m/s
   h) 4 m/s
   i) 5.31 m/s
   j) 6 m/s

4.5.7.2 Conservation of Momentum (HT only)

1. Define "momentum".
2. How is momentum calculated?
3. What is meant by "a closed system"?
4. What is meant by conservation of momentum?
5. In terms of momentum, what is:
   a) An elastic collision?
   b) An inelastic collision?
   c) An explosion?

6a) A car of mass 3000 kg travelling at 25m/s collides with a van of mass 1000 kg travelling at 10m/s in the same direction. They move together after the collision. What is their velocity after the collision?

b) A car of mass 3000 kg travelling at 17m/s collides with a van of mass 2000 kg travelling at 8m/s in the same direction. They move together after the collision. What is their velocity after the collision?

c) A car of mass 3000 kg travelling at 8m/s collides with a van of mass 2000 kg travelling at 20m/s in the same direction. They move together after the collision. What is their velocity after the collision?

d) A car of mass 2000 kg travelling at 6m/s collides with a van of mass 1000 kg travelling at 20m/s in the same direction. They move together after the collision. What is their velocity after the collision?

e) A car of mass 2000 kg travelling at 15m/s collides with a van of mass 2000 kg travelling at 24m/s in the same direction. They move together after the collision. What is their velocity after the collision?

f) A car of mass 2000 kg travelling at 11m/s collides with a van of mass 3000 kg travelling at 4m/s in the same direction. They move together after the collision. What is their velocity after the collision?

g) A car of mass 3000 kg travelling at 7m/s collides with a van of mass 1000 kg travelling at 22m/s in the same direction. They move together after the collision. What is their velocity after the collision?

h) A car of mass 1000 kg travelling at 18m/s collides with a van of mass 2000 kg travelling at 1m/s in the same direction. They move together after the collision. What is their velocity after the collision?

i) A car of mass 2000 kg travelling at 22m/s collides with a van of mass 2000 kg travelling at 17m/s in the same direction. They move together after the collision. What is their velocity after the collision?

j) A car of mass 3000 kg travelling at 21m/s collides with a van of mass 2000 kg travelling at 21m/s in the same direction. They move together after the collision. What is their velocity after the collision?

7a) A 800 kg cannon fires a shell of mass 90 kg at a velocity of 11m/s. Determine the recoil velocity of the cannon.

b) A 200 kg cannon fires a shell of mass 90 kg at a velocity of 11m/s. Determine the recoil velocity of the cannon.

c) A 600 kg cannon fires a shell of mass 30 kg at a velocity of 22m/s. Determine the recoil velocity of the cannon.

d) A 700 kg cannon fires a shell of mass 60 kg at a velocity of 4m/s. Determine the recoil velocity of the cannon.

e) A 600 kg cannon fires a shell of mass 30 kg at a velocity of 21m/s. Determine the recoil velocity of the cannon.

f) A 500 kg cannon fires a shell of mass 30 kg at a velocity of 15m/s. Determine the recoil velocity of the cannon.

g) A 300 kg cannon fires a shell of mass 10 kg at a velocity of 12m/s. Determine the recoil velocity of the cannon.

h) A 500 kg cannon fires a shell of mass 60 kg at a velocity of 13m/s. Determine the recoil velocity of the cannon.

i) A 300 kg cannon fires a shell of mass 60 kg at a velocity of 7m/s. Determine the recoil velocity of the cannon.

j) A 500 kg cannon fires a shell of mass 70 kg at a velocity of 1m/s. Determine the recoil velocity of the cannon.

4.5.7.2 Conservation of Momentum (HT only) Answers

1. Momentum is mass x velocity
2. As above
3. No energy is lost or gained
4. Momentum before a collision or explosion is the same as that after.
5.
    a) One where the two objects do not stick together eg snooker balls
    b) One where the two objects stick together eg trains and carriages
    c) One where two objects fly apart eg cannon and cannonball

6
a) 21 m/s
b) 13 m/s
c) 13 m/s
d) 11 m/s
e) 20 m/s
f) 6.8 m/s
g) 11 m/s
h) 6.7 m/s
i) 20 m/s
j) 21 m/s

7
a) 1.2 m/s
b) 5 m/s
c) 1.1 m/s
d) 0.34 m/s
e) 1.1 m/s
f) 0.9 m/s
g) 0.4 m/s
h) 1.6 m/s
i) 1.4 m/s
j) 0.14 m/s

4.5.7.3 Changes in Momentum (physics only)

$$F = \frac{m \, \Delta v}{\Delta t}$$

(Students should be able to apply this equation which is given on the *Physics Equation Sheet.*)
Give all answers to 2 significant figures.

1a) An object of mass 9 kg accelerates from 6 m/s to 22 m/s in 0.075 s. What is the force acting?

b) An object of mass 3 kg accelerates from 6 m/s to 13 m/s in 0.086 s. What is the force acting?

c) An object of mass 2 kg accelerates from 8 m/s to 11 m/s in 0.078 s. What is the force acting?

d) An object of mass 6 kg accelerates from 7 m/s to 14 m/s in 0.018 s. What is the force acting?

e) An object of mass 9 kg accelerates from 8 m/s to 14 m/s in 0.096 s. What is the force acting?

f) An object of mass 4 kg accelerates from 1 m/s to 14 m/s in 0.071 s. What is the force acting?

g) An object of mass 8 kg accelerates from 2 m/s to 21 m/s in 0.057 s. What is the force acting?

h) An object of mass 3 kg accelerates from 7 m/s to 24 m/s in 0.05 s. What is the force acting?

i) An object of mass 7 kg accelerates from 4 m/s to 18 m/s in 0.016 s. What is the force acting?

j) An object of mass 7 kg accelerates from 10 m/s to 20 m/s in 0.066 s. What is the force acting?

2a) What is the change in momentum caused by a force of 70 N acting for 0.075 s?

b) What is the change in momentum caused by a force of 2000 N acting for 0.013 s?

c) What is the change in momentum caused by a force of 800 N acting for 0.085 s?

d) What is the change in momentum caused by a force of 80 N acting for 0.077 s?

e) What is the change in momentum caused by a force of 20 N acting for 0.096 s?

f) What is the change in momentum caused by a force of 30 N acting for 0.055 s?

g) What is the change in momentum caused by a force of 50000 N acting for 0.038 s?

h) What is the change in momentum caused by a force of 40 N acting for 0.085 s?

i) What is the change in momentum caused by a force of 70000 N acting for 0.007 s?

j) What is the change in momentum caused by a force of 5000 N acting for 0.019 s?

3a) For what length of time must a 70000 N act to make the momentum of an object change by 40 kgm/s?

b) For what length of time must a 900 N act to make the momentum of an object change by 40 kgm/s?

c) For what length of time must a 40 N act to make the momentum of an object change by 90 kgm/s?

d) For what length of time must a 30000 N act to make the momentum of an object change by 20 kgm/s?

e) For what length of time must a 10000 N act to make the momentum of an object change by 70 kgm/s?

f) For what length of time must a 1000 N act to make the momentum of an object change by 70 kgm/s?

g) For what length of time must a 1000 N act to make the momentum of an object change by 10 kgm/s?

h) For what length of time must a 500 N act to make the momentum of an object change by 40 kgm/s?

i) For what length of time must a 70000 N act to make the momentum of an object change by 90 kgm/s?

j) For what length of time must a 4000 N act to make the momentum of an object change by 80 kgm/s?

4a) What is the final velocity when a force of 5000 N acts for 0.094 s on a body travelling at 2 m/s?

b) What is the final velocity when a force of 2000 N acts for 0.064 s on a body travelling at 6 m/s?

c) What is the final velocity when a force of 20000 N acts for 0.002 s on a body travelling at 1 m/s?

d) What is the final velocity when a force of 600 N acts for 0.024 s on a body travelling at 8 m/s?

e) What is the final velocity when a force of 80000 N acts for 0.05 s on a body travelling at 3 m/s?

f) What is the final velocity when a force of 900 N acts for 0.075 s on a body travelling at 3 m/s?

g) What is the final velocity when a force of 900 N acts for 0.048 s on a body travelling at 1 m/s?

h) What is the final velocity when a force of 60000 N acts for 0.088 s on a body travelling at 9 m/s?

i) What is the final velocity when a force of 900 N acts for 0.068 s on a body travelling at 4 m/s?

j) What is the final velocity when a force of 100 N acts for 0.079 s on a body travelling at 8 m/s?

5a) What is the initial velocity when a force of 4590 N acts for 0.0058 s to make a body reach 90 m/s?

b) What is the initial velocity when a force of 4772 N acts for 0.0093 s to make a body reach 96 m/s?

c) What is the initial velocity when a force of 2771 N acts for 0.0054 s to make a body reach 100 m/s?

d) What is the initial velocity when a force of 4956 N acts for 0.0082 s to make a body reach 69 m/s?

e) What is the initial velocity when a force of 3971 N acts for 0.0074 s to make a body reach 82 m/s?

f) What is the initial velocity when a force of 4607 N acts for 0.0083 s to make a body reach 74 m/s?

g) What is the initial velocity when a force of 2341 N acts for 0.0072 s to make a body reach 80 m/s?

h) What is the initial velocity when a force of 3122 N acts for 0.008 s to make a body reach 60 m/s?

i) What is the initial velocity when a force of 1284 N acts for 0.0046 s to make a body reach 85 m/s?

j) What is the initial velocity when a force of 1264 N acts for 0.0079 s to make a body reach 88 m/s?

4.5.7.3 Changes in Momentum (physics only) Answers

1a) 1900 N
b) 240 N
c) 77 N
d) 2300 N
e) 560 N
f) 730 N
g) 2700 N
h) 1000 N
i) 6100 N
j) 1100 N

4a) 470m/s
b) 130m/s
c) 41m/s
d) 22m/s
e) 4000m/s
f) 71m/s
g) 44m/s
h) 5300m/s
i) 65m/s
j) 16m/s

2a) 5.3 kgm/s
b) 26 kgm/s
c) 68 kgm/s
d) 6.2 kgm/s
e) 1.9 kgm/s
f) 1.7 kgm/s
g) 1900 kgm/s
h) 3.4 kgm/s
i) 490 kgm/s
j) 95 kgm/s

5a) 63m/s
b) 52m/s
c) 85m/s
d) 28m/s
e) 53m/s
f) 36m/s
g) 63m/s
h) 35m/s
i) 79m/s
j) 78m/s

3a) 0.00057 s
b) 0.044 s
c) 2.3 s
d) 0.00067 s
e) 0.007 s
f) 0.07 s
g) 0.01 s
h) 0.08 s
i) 0.0013 s
j) 0.02 s

4.6.1.1 Transverse and Longitudinal Waves and 4.6.1.2 Properties of Waves

1. What is the definition of a wave?
2. A buoy sits on the surface of the water as the waves go by in front of him from left to right.
   a) Which way do the waves move?
   b) Which way does the buoy move?
   c) How does this example explain the nature of waves?
3. Sketch a transverse wave. On your wave label:
   a) A crest
   b) A trough
   c) The amplitude
   d) The wavelength
4. Define the frequency of a wave.
5. Give 3 examples of waves which are transverse.
6. Describe a longitudinal wave.
7. What is a compression?
8. What is a rarefaction?
9. How can the wavelength of a longitudinal wave be determined?
10. Give 2 examples of longitudinal waves.
11. Define the time period of a wave in words.

$$\text{period} = \frac{1}{\text{frequency}}$$

$$T = \frac{1}{f}$$

(Students should be able to apply this equation which is given on the Physics Equation Sheet.)
Give all answers to 2 significant figures.

1. Find the Time Period when the frequency is:
   a) 1 Hz
   b) 20 Hz
   c) 50 Hz
   d) 0.1 Hz
   e) 0.02 Hz
   f) 40 kHz
   g) 100 kHz
   h) 1 MHz
   i) 4 mHz

2. Calculate the Frequency when the time period is:
   a) 1 s
   b) 10 s
   c) 100 s
   d) 0.5 s
   e) 0.08 s
   f) 0.0004 s
   g) 1 minute
   h) 1 hour
   i) 0.125 hours

4.6.1.1 Transverse and Longitudinal Waves and 4.6.1.2 Properties of Waves Answers

1. A wave is a vibration or disturbance transmitted through a material (a medium) or through space. Waves transfer energy and information from one place to another, but they do not transfer material.

2.
   a) Horizontally, left to right
   b) Up and down
   c) In these transverse waves, the energy (wave) move from left to right but the "particles" (medium) moves up and down

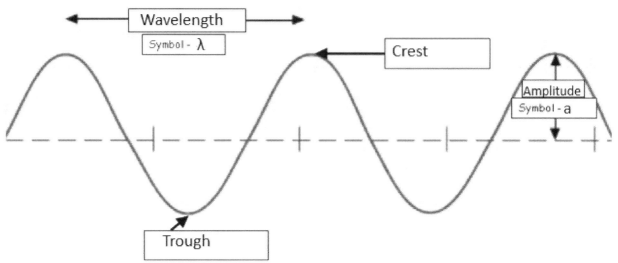

3.
4. The number of complete waves passing a point in one second.
5. Light, water, s waves (seismic), etc
6. A series of compressions and rarefactions in a medium
7. Where the particles are closer together than their rest position
8. Where the particles are further apart than their rest position
9. Measure the distance from the centre of one compression (or rarefaction) to the centre of the next one
10. Sound, p waves (seismic), etc
11. The time taken for one complete cycle.

1.
    a) 1s
    b) 0.05s
    c) 0.02s
    d) 10s
    e) 50s
    f) 2.5×10^{-5} s
    g) 1×10^{-5} s
    h) 1×10^{-6} s
    i) 250s

2.
    a) 1 Hz
    b) 0.1 Hz
    c) 0.01 Hz
    d) 2 Hz
    e) 12.5 Hz
    f) 2500 Hz
    g) 0.017 Hz
    h) 0.00028 Hz
    i) 0.0022 Hz

Wave Speed = frequency x wavelength

v = f λ

(Students should be able to recall and apply this equation.)

Give all answers to 2 significant figures.

1a) A wave of frequency 400000000 Hz has a wavelength of 8.1 m. Calculate its speed.
b) A wave of frequency 900000000 Hz has a wavelength of 8.14 m. Calculate its speed.
c) A wave of frequency 10000000 Hz has a wavelength of 5.02 m. Calculate its speed.
d) A wave of frequency 70000 Hz has a wavelength of 8.06 m. Calculate its speed.
e) A wave of frequency 1000000 Hz has a wavelength of 5.34 m. Calculate its speed.
f) A wave of frequency 900000 Hz has a wavelength of 6.55 m. Calculate its speed.
g) A wave of frequency 200000000 Hz has a wavelength of 0.22 m. Calculate its speed.
h) A wave of frequency 8000 Hz has a wavelength of 5.87 m. Calculate its speed.
i) A wave of frequency 2000000 Hz has a wavelength of 5.88 m. Calculate its speed.
j) A wave of frequency 10000 Hz has a wavelength of 5.43 m. Calculate its speed.

2a) A wave of frequency 100 Hz is travelling at 6.91 m/s. Determine its wavelength.
b) A wave of frequency 3000 Hz is travelling at 8.47 m/s. Determine its wavelength.
c) A wave of frequency 900 Hz is travelling at 8.01 m/s. Determine its wavelength.
d) A wave of frequency 900000 Hz is travelling at 2.93 m/s. Determine its wavelength.
e) A wave of frequency 8000 Hz is travelling at 5.62 m/s. Determine its wavelength.
f) A wave of frequency 300000 Hz is travelling at 1.81 m/s. Determine its wavelength.
g) A wave of frequency 1000 Hz is travelling at 6 m/s. Determine its wavelength.
h) A wave of frequency 9000 Hz is travelling at 3.64 m/s. Determine its wavelength.
i) A wave of frequency 300000 Hz is travelling at 5.47 m/s. Determine its wavelength.
j) A wave of frequency 20 Hz is travelling at 0.71 m/s. Determine its wavelength.

3a) A wave of wavelength 2.52 m.is travelling at 7.18 m/s. Find its frequency.
b) A wave of wavelength 4.43 m.is travelling at 8.59 m/s. Find its frequency.
c) A wave of wavelength 0.37 m.is travelling at 0.24 m/s. Find its frequency.
d) A wave of wavelength 2.3 m.is travelling at 3.1 m/s. Find its frequency.
e) A wave of wavelength 1.45 m.is travelling at 8.17 m/s. Find its frequency.
f) A wave of wavelength 6.43 m.is travelling at 5.31 m/s. Find its frequency.
g) A wave of wavelength 6.35 m.is travelling at 7.35 m/s. Find its frequency.
h) A wave of wavelength 4.84 m.is travelling at 5.99 m/s. Find its frequency.
i) A wave of wavelength 0.88 m.is travelling at 5.87 m/s. Find its frequency.
j) A wave of wavelength 3.47 m.is travelling at 8.67 m/s. Find its frequency.

4a) What is the wavelength of an electromagnetic wave of frequency 3000000 Hz?
b) What is the wavelength of an electromagnetic wave of frequency 500000 Hz?
c) What is the wavelength of an electromagnetic wave of frequency 40000000 Hz?
d) What is the wavelength of an electromagnetic wave of frequency 1000000000 Hz?
e) What is the wavelength of an electromagnetic wave of frequency 900000 Hz?
f) What is the frequency of an electromagnetic wave of wavelength 0.6 m?
g) What is the frequency of an electromagnetic wave of wavelength 4.7 m?
h) What is the frequency of an electromagnetic wave of wavelength 6.9 m?
i) What is the frequency of an electromagnetic wave of wavelength 2.6 m?

j) What is the frequency of an electromagnetic wave of wavelength 7.9 m?

5a) Calculate the speed of a wave with a wavelength of 3.1 m and a frequency of 3.8 Hz
b) Determine the frequency of a wave with a wavelength of 2.4 m and a speed of 10 m/s
c) Calculate the speed of a water wave with a wavelength of 6 m and a frequency of 2.4 Hz
d) Find the wavelength of a water wave with a speed of 1.6 m/s and a frequency of 8.7 Hz
e) Find the wavelength of a wave with a speed of 2.7 m/s and a frequency of 9.5 Hz
f) Calculate the wavelength of a wave with a speed of 4.2 m/s and a frequency of 1.7 Hz
g) Calculate the wavelength of a wave with a speed of 7.9 m/s and a frequency of 8.2 Hz
h) Find the speed of a wave with a wavelength of 0.3 m and a frequency of 6.5 Hz
i) Find the speed of a wave with a wavelength of 2.3 m and a frequency of 3 Hz
j) Determine the frequency of a water wave with a wavelength of 6.1 m and a speed of 3.5 m/s

Wave Speed = frequency x wavelength Answers

1a) 3200000000 m/s
b) 7300000000 m/s
c) 50000000 m/s
d) 560000 m/s
e) 5300000 m/s
f) 5900000 m/s
g) 44000000 m/s
h) 47000 m/s
i) 12000000 m/s
j) 54000 m/s

2a) 0.069 m
b) 0.0028 m
c) 0.0089 m
d) 0.0000033 m
e) 0.0007 m
f) 0.000006 m
g) 0.006 m
h) 0.0004 m
i) 0.000018 m
j) 0.036 m

3a) 2.8 Hz
b) 1.9 Hz
c) 0.65 Hz
d) 1.3 Hz
e) 5.6 Hz
f) 0.83 Hz
g) 1.2 Hz
h) 1.2 Hz
i) 6.7 Hz
j) 2.5 Hz

4a) 100 m
b) 600 m
c) 7.5 m
d) 0.3 m
e) 330 m
f) 500000000 Hz
g) 64000000 Hz
h) 43000000 Hz
i) 120000000 Hz
j) 38000000 Hz

5a) 12 m/s
b) 4.2 Hz
c) 14 m/s
d) 0.18 m
e) 0.28 m
f) 2.5 m
g) 0.96 m
h) 2 m/s
i) 6.9 m/s
j) 0.57 Hz

4.6.1.3 Reflection of waves (physics only)

1. Define "Reflection".
2. What is a Normal Line?
3. What is the Law of Reflection?
4. Water waves are hitting a harbour wall at an angle and are reflected. Draw a diagram to show what is happening.
5. What is meant by transmission?
6. What is meant by absorption?
7. What happens to the energy of the absorbed waves?
8. Light is shone onto the surface of a glass bottle. Some of the light is reflected. What happens to the remainder of the light? Draw a diagram to help your description.

4.6.1.3 Reflection of Waves (physics only) Answers

1. Reflection is the change in direction of a wave at a boundary between two different media, so that the wave moves back into the medium it came from.
2. A line at 90° to the surface of a medium
3. The angle of incidence = the angle of reflection
4. Suitable diagram showing waves incident and reflected at the same angle
5. When a wave passes through a medium
6. When waves are taken in by the medium and not reflected or transmitted
7. They increase the temperature of the medium
8. Suitable diagram showing a proportion of the incident waves reflected, refracted and transmitted and some absorbed.

4.6.1.4 Sound Waves (physics only) (HT only)

1. What are sound waves?
2. Are sound waves Longitudinal or Transverse?
3. What can sound waves travel through?
4. What can sound waves not travel through?
5. Explain how sound waves travel through a solid.
6. Explain how sound waves are detected in the human ear.
7. Explain the roles of the following parts of the ear:
   a) Pinna
   b) Ear Canal
   c) Ear Wax
   d) Ear Drum
   e) Ossicles
   f) Cochlea
   g) Auditory Nerve
   h) Semi-circular Canals
8. Name the three Ossicles.
9. Explain why your voice sounds differently when you hear it to when someone else hears it.
10. What is the range of human hearing?

4.6.1.4 Sound Waves (physics only) (HT only) Answers

1. A series of compressions and rarefactions passing through the air.
2. Longitudinal
3. Most media (eg air, water, metal, etc)
4. A Vacuum, empty space, etc
5. A series of compressions and rarefactions
6. Sound waves channelled in to the ear. Causes eardrum to vibrate. This causes ossicles to vibrate. Vibrations passed into the cochlea so small hairs inside it vibrate. Converted into an electrical signal. Passed through auditory nerve to brain.
7.
    a) Funnels sound waves into Ear canal.
    b) Sound travels along to the ear drum
    c) Wax traps particles/bacteria/pathogens etc
    d) Vibrates and causes ossicles to vibrate
    e) Vibrate and amplify the vibration. Pass vibrations onto the cochlea
    f) Contains tiny hairs which vibrate at certain frequencies. Change vibrations to electrical signals
    g) Transmits electrical impulses to brain
    h) Behave like spirit levels and are part of our sense of balance
8. Hammer, Anvil and Stirrup
9. Someone else hears just the sound reaching their ears. You hear both the external sound and the sound internally via the back of your mouth.
10. 20 to 20000 Hz

4.6.1.5 Waves for Detection and Exploration (physics only) (HT only)

Material	Speed of Sound [m/s]
Air	340
Rubber	60
Lead	1210
Gold	3240
Glass	4540
Copper	4600
Aluminium	6320
Water	1500
Iron	5800
Brass	4700

1. Describe how Ultrasound waves can be used to make an image of an unborn baby in the womb.
2. Explain why Ultrasound waves are used instead of X Rays.
3. Explain the differences between S and P Seismic waves.
4. Explain how detection of S and P waves in different locations has led to a greater understanding of the internal structure of the Earth.
5. Fishing boats use Echo Sounding to locate fish. Explain how this is done.
6. Bats use Echo Location to locate prey and for navigation. Explain how this is done.

7a) The echo of an Ultrasound wave returns after 0.5 ms when travelling through Water. How far did the Ultrasound wave travel? How far away was the surface off which it reflected?

b) The echo of an Ultrasound wave returns after 2.1 ms when travelling through Rubber. How far did the Ultrasound wave travel? How far away was the surface off which it reflected?

c) The echo of an Ultrasound wave returns after 9.3 ms when travelling through Aluminium. How far did the Ultrasound wave travel? How far away was the surface off which it reflected?

d) The echo of an Ultrasound wave returns after 6.7 ms when travelling through Gold. How far did the Ultrasound wave travel? How far away was the surface off which it reflected?

e) The echo of an Ultrasound wave returns after 8.3 ms when travelling through Copper. How far did the Ultrasound wave travel? How far away was the surface off which it reflected?

f) The echo of an Ultrasound wave returns after 1 ms when travelling through Glass. How far did the Ultrasound wave travel? How far away was the surface off which it reflected?

g) The echo of an Ultrasound wave returns after 7.2 ms when travelling through Glass. How far did the Ultrasound wave travel? How far away was the surface off which it reflected?

h) The echo of an Ultrasound wave returns after 5.3 ms when travelling through Brass. How far did the Ultrasound wave travel? How far away was the surface off which it reflected?

i) The echo of an Ultrasound wave returns after 4.3 ms when travelling through Rubber. How far did the Ultrasound wave travel? How far away was the surface off which it reflected?

j) The echo of an Ultrasound wave returns after 4.9 ms when travelling through Brass. How far did the Ultrasound wave travel? How far away was the surface off which it reflected?

8a) An echo of an Ultrasound wave travels 93 m in Aluminium. How long did this take in milliseconds?

b) An echo of an Ultrasound wave travels 20 m in Lead. How long did this take in milliseconds?

c) An echo of an Ultrasound wave travels 74 m in Aluminium. How long did this take in milliseconds?

d) An echo of an Ultrasound wave travels 44 m in Iron. How long did this take in milliseconds?

e) An echo of an Ultrasound wave travels 28 m in Brass. How long did this take in milliseconds?

f) An echo of an Ultrasound wave travels 43 m in Lead. How long did this take in milliseconds?

g) An echo of an Ultrasound wave travels 74 m in Brass. How long did this take in milliseconds?

h) An echo of an Ultrasound wave travels 35 m in Iron. How long did this take in milliseconds?

i) An echo of an Ultrasound wave travels 34 m in Lead. How long did this take in milliseconds?

j) An echo of an Ultrasound wave travels 77 m in Rubber. How long did this take in milliseconds?

4.6.1.5 Waves for Detection and Exploration (physics only) (HT only) Answers

1. Ultrasound waves are generated and the body is exposed to them. They pass through the skin and are reflected off the surface of the baby. They reflect back to the detector and an image is formed.
2. Non-ionising. Cause no damage to cells/DNA
3. S waves are transverse, P waves are longitudinal
4. S waves cannot pass through liquids. There are therefore regions of the earth where they are not detected. Therefore conclusions can be drawn as to how the waves have passed from the point at which the earthquake is to the detectors all around the earth.
5. Boat emits an ultrasound pulse. The sound is reflected off a shoal of fish. The resulting echo is detected on the boat. The time it takes determines the position of the fish.
6. Bat emits a high pitched sound pulse. The sound is reflected off the prey/wall/etc. The resulting echo is detected by the bat. The time it takes determines the position of the object and the bat reacts accordingly.

7a) 0.75 m   0.375 m
b) 130 m   65 m
c) 59000 m   29500 m
d) 22000 m   11000 m
e) 38000 m   19000 m
f) 4500 m   2250 m
g) 33 m   16.5 m
h) 25 m   12.5 m
i) 0.26 m   0.13 m
j) 23 m   11.5 m

8a) 15 ms
b) 17 ms
c) 12 ms
d) 7.6 ms
e) 6 ms
f) 36 ms
g) 16 ms
h) 6 ms
i) 28 ms
j) 1300 ms

4.6.2.1 Types of Electromagnetic Waves and
4.6.2.4 Uses and Applications of Electromagnetic Waves

1. Are Electromagnetic Waves transverse or longitudinal?
2. What are the seven regions of the electromagnetic spectrum?
3. Which region of the electromagnetic spectrum:
   a) has the longest wavelength?
   b) has the shortest wavelength?
   c) has the highest frequency?
   d) has the lowest frequency?
   e) has the greatest speed?
   f) is detected by our eyes?
4. What are the uses of:
   a) Radio Waves.
   Explain why Radio Waves are suitable for this application.
   b) Microwaves.
   Explain why Microwaves are suitable for this application.
   c) Infrared Waves.
   Explain why Infrared Waves are suitable for this application.
   d) Visible Light.
   Explain why Visible Light is suitable for this application.
   e) Ultraviolet.
   Explain why Ultraviolet is suitable for this application.
   f) X-Rays.
   Explain why X-Rays are suitable for this application.
   g) Gamma Rays.
   Explain why Gamma Rays are suitable for this application.
5. Which regions are dangerous to human beings and why?

4.6.2.1 Types of Electromagnetic Waves and 4.6.2.4 Uses and Applications of Electromagnetic Waves Answers

1. Transverse
2. Radio, Microwave, Infra Red, Visible, Ultraviolet, X rays, Gamma
3.
    a) Radio
    b) Gamma
    c) Gamma
    d) Radio
    e) All same speed
    f) Visible
4.
    a) Communication. Long wavelength, low frequency, safe, can be reflected off ionosphere
    b) Communication with satellites, Pass through ionosphere
    c) Heating. Causes material to vibrate.
    d) Optical devices. Can be detected by our eyes
    e) Security marking. Invisible normally but can be seen under UV lights
    f) Internal imaging. Can pass through soft but not hard tissues.
    g) Sterilisation and Killing Cancerous cells. Kills pathogens and damages DNA of cancerous cells.
5. Visible – Intense lights (eg sun and lasers) can damage eyes
   UV, X Rays and Gamma – Ionising radiation can cause cancers (eg skin cancer from UV)

4.6.2.2 Properties of Electromagnetic Waves 1

1. Define Absorbance.
2. Explain the effects that absorbance of incident electromagnetic waves may have on an object.
3. Define Transmission.
4. Define Reflection.
5. Visible light is incident upon a piece of clear glass. Draw a diagram showing absorbance, transmittance and reflection of the light in, on and through the glass.
6. What changes could be made to the glass to alter the percentages of the light which are absorbed, transmitted and reflected?
7. Explain how the nature of the surface affects how light is absorbed or reflected.
8. Define Refraction.
9. Draw a diagram to show refraction of light waves as they enter, pass through and then leave a glass block.
10. What causes refraction of light?

4.6.2.2 Properties of Electromagnetic Waves 1 Answers

1. The capacity of a material to absorb light of a specified wavelength.
2. Increase temperature of a material
3. Transmission of light is the movement of electromagnetic waves through a material.
4. Reflection is the change in direction of a wave at a boundary between two different media, so that the wave moves back into the medium it came from.
5. Suitable diagram showing a proportion of the incident waves reflected, refracted and transmitted and some absorbed.
6. The more that is absorbed, the warmer it will become.
7. Light, shiny surfaces reflect more. Dark, matt surfaces absorb more.
8. Refraction is due to the difference in velocity of the waves in different substances.
9. Suitable diagram showing the normal, angle of incidence, angle of refraction and the boundary between the two media
10. Change in velocity

4.6.2.3 Properties of Electromagnetic Waves 2

1. How are Radio waves produced?
2. How are Radio waves detected?
3. How are Gamma waves produced?
4. What hazardous effects can Ultraviolet waves have on the human body?
5. What can be done to prevent these effects?
6. What hazardous effects can X-Rays have on the human body?
7. What can be done to prevent these effects?
8. What hazardous effects can Gamma waves have on the human body?
9. What can be done to prevent these effects?
10. The effect of radiation on the body depends on 2 things. What are they?
11. What is the definition of Radiation Dose?
12. What is the unit of Radiation Dose?
13. Make a list if professions and/or locations where you would expect radiation dose to be higher than usual.

4.6.2.3 Properties of electromagnetic waves 2 Answers

1. Radio waves can be produced by oscillations in electrical circuits.
2. Radio waves can be absorbed by a piece of metal eg an aerial. They produce an alternating current with the same frequency of the radio wave itself.
3. Gamma rays are produced by changes in the nucleus of an atom
4. Premature aging, skin cancer or similar response.
5. Sun cream, cover the body (clothing) staying indoors, etc
6. Mutation of genes and cancer
7. Limiting exposure, protective screens (lead lined), monitoring
8. Mutation of genes and cancer
9. Limiting exposure, protective screens and clothing (lead lined), monitoring
10. The type of radiation and the size of the dose
11. A measure of the risk of harm resulting from an exposure of the body to the radiation.
12. Sievert, millisievert
13. Pilot, radiographer, etc

4.6.2.5 Lenses (physics only)

$$\text{magnification} = \frac{\text{image height}}{\text{object height}}$$

Students should be able to apply this equation which is given on the *Physics equation sheet*.
Give all answers to 2 significant figures.

1a) What is the magnification of a lens when the object height is 8.3m and image height 2.9m?
b) What is the magnification of a lens when the object height is 6.6m and image height 9.6m?
c) What is the magnification of a lens when the object height is 4.8m and image height 4.8m?
d) What is the magnification of a lens when the object height is 0.7m and image height 0.6m?
e) What is the magnification of a lens when the object height is 0.7m and image height 9.8m?
f) What is the magnification of a lens when the object height is 1m and image height 8.3m?
g) What is the magnification of a lens when the object height is 9.8mm and image height 7.1cm?
h) What is the magnification of a lens when the object height is 8.1mm and image height 9.7m?
i) What is the magnification of a lens when the object height is 5.8m and image height 3.8m?
j) What is the magnification of a lens when the object height is 8.8cm and image height 9.6cm?

2a) Determine the object height of a lens with magnification 4.4 and image height 4.1m.
b) Determine the object height of a lens with magnification 0.7 and image height 9.3m.
c) Determine the object height of a lens with magnification 7.8 and image height 9.9m.
d) Determine the object height of a lens with magnification 6.2 and image height 5.2m.
e) Determine the object height of a lens with magnification 0.9 and image height 0.8m.
f) Determine the object height of a lens with magnification 9 and image height 7.7m.
g) Determine the object height of a lens with magnification 3.8 and image height 8.8m
h) Determine the object height of a lens with magnification 7.2 and image height 6.2m
i) Determine the object height of a lens with magnification 1.4 and image height 1.8mm
j) Determine the object height of a lens with magnification 7.3 and image height 8.8m

3a) Find the image height of a lens with magnification 7.4 and object height 7m.
b) Find the image height of a lens with magnification 6.9 and object height 3.4m.
c) Find the image height of a lens with magnification 7.7 and object height 4.4m.
d) Find the image height of a lens with magnification 3.8 and object height 5.5m.
e) Find the image height of a lens with magnification 2.4 and object height 2.3m.
f) Find the image height of a lens with magnification 3.5 and object height 6.2m.
g) Find the image height of a lens with magnification 6.1 and object height 1.5m
h) Find the image height of a lens with magnification 5.2 and object height 4.6mm
i) Find the image height of a lens with magnification 0.5 and object height 7.3m
j) Find the image height of a lens with magnification 3.1 and object height 4.3cm

4.6.2.5 Lenses (physics only) Answers

1a) 0.35
b) 1.5
c) 1
d) 0.86
e) 14
f) 8.3
g) 7.2
h) 1200
i) 0.66
j) 1.1

2a) 0.93 m
b) 13 m
c) 1.3 m
d) 0.84 m
e) 0.89 m
f) 0.86 m
g) 2.3 m
h) 0.86 m
i) 1.3 mm
j) 1.2 m

3a) 5 2m
b) 23 m
c) 34 m
d) 21 m
e) 5.5 m
f) 22 m
g) 9.2 m
h) 24 mm
i) 3.7 m
j) 13 cm

4.6.2.6 Visible Light (physics only)

1. List the colours of visible light in the Electromagnetic Spectrum.
2. Which colour of light has the longest wavelength?
3. Which colour of light has the shortest wavelength?
4. Define Specular Reflection. Give an example with a diagram.
5. Define Diffuse Reflection. Give an example with a diagram.
6. Describe how colour filters work.
7. Use a labelled diagram to explain:
   a) how a filter produces green light.
   b) how a filter produces blue light.
   c) how a filter produces red light.
   d) how a combination of 2 filters can prevent any light from being transmitted.
8. Define the word "Opaque".
9. Use a labelled diagram to explain:
   a) why a red object appears red under white light.
   b) why a blue object appears blue under white light.
   c) why a red object appears red under red light.
   d) why a green object appears green under green light.
   e) why a white object appears white under white light.
   f) why a black object appears black under white light.
   g) why a red object appears black under blue light.
   h) why a blue object appears black under green light.
10. What does transparent mean?
11. What does translucent mean?
12. An opaque object is more likely to heat up in bright light than a transparent object. Explain this observation in terms of transmittance and absorbance.
13. It is sometimes important to cut out all light from an area. Explain how coloured filters can be used to do this.
14. Beer can go off if exposed to too much light. Explain why beer is often stored in brown glasses rather than clear ones. Use a diagram to explain your answer.
15. Photosynthesising plants contain chlorophyll which appears green. In greenhouses and polytunnels, farmers often use red light to improve growth of plants. Explain this use of light and illustrate with an appropriate diagram.

4.6.2.6 Visible Light (physics only) Answers

1. ROYGBIV
2. Red
3. Violet
4. Reflection from a smooth surface in a single direction. Suitable Diagram
5. Reflection from a rough surface showing scattering
6. Light of many frequencies/wavelengths/colours is incident upon a filter. Most colours are absorbed, one is transmitted.
7.
   a) Suitable diagram showing ROYGBIV incident and only green transmitted. Comment on absorbed light.
   b) Suitable diagram showing ROYGBIV incident and only blue transmitted Comment on absorbed light.
   c) Suitable diagram showing ROYGBIV incident and only red transmitted Comment on absorbed light.
   d) Suitable diagram showing ROYGBIV incident and only one colour transmitted through the first filter and then nothing through second filter. Comment on absorbed light.
8. Does not allow light to pass through it.
9.
   a) Suitable diagram showing ROYGBIV incident and only red reflected. Comment on absorbed light.
   b) Suitable diagram showing ROYGBIV incident and only blue reflected. Comment on absorbed light.
   c) Suitable diagram showing Red light incident and only red reflected. Comment on absorbed light.
   d) Suitable diagram showing Green light incident and only green reflected. Comment on absorbed light.
   e) Suitable diagram showing ROYGBIV incident and all light reflected. Comment on absorbed light.
   f) Suitable diagram showing ROYGBIV incident and no light reflected. Comment on absorbed light.
   g) Suitable diagram showing Blue light incident and no light reflected. Comment on absorbed light.
   h) Suitable diagram showing Green light incident and no light reflected. Comment on absorbed light.
10. Allows light to be transmitted
11. Allows some light to be transmitted
12. No light is transmitted, all is absorbed in an opaque object.
13. 2 different coloured filters will cut out all light. Suitable diagram to show this.
14. Brown glass absorbs more and transmits less light. Suitable diagram showing this.
15. Leaves absorb red light and reflect green light. Suitable diagram.

4.6.3 Black Body Radiation (consisting 4.6.3.1 Emission and Absorption of Infrared Radiation and 4.6.3.2 Perfect Black Bodies and Radiation) (physics only)

1. Which region of the Electromagnetic Spectrum is most closely associated with absorption and emission of heat?
2. How does a body become hotter?
3. How does a body become cooler?
4. What is the definition of a Perfect Black Body?
5. How does a body maintain constant temperature?
6. List and explain the factors which affect the temperature of the Earth.
7. Sketch graphs to show the range of wavelengths emitted for:
   a) A very hot body
   b) A cooler body
8. Explain how astronomers can estimate the temperature of a distant star.

4.6.3 Black Body Radiation (consisting 4.6.3.1 Emission and Absorption of Infrared Radiation and 4.6.3.2 Perfect Black Bodies and Radiation) (physics only)

Answers

1. IR
2. By absorbing radiation
3. By emitting radiation
4. Black bodies are perfect absorbers and emitters of radiation
5. When the energy emitted and absorbed are equal
6. Composition of the atmosphere (eg concentrations of greenhouse gases – water vapour, methane, carbon dioxide), rates at which light/radiation/infra red are absorbed and emitted by the earth's surface and atmosphere.
7.

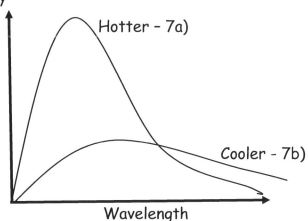

8. Observe the spectrum of the distant star. Compare the peak wavelength to the graph and use the comparison to estimate the temperature.

4.7.1.1 Poles of a Magnet and 4.7.1.2 Magnetic Fields

1. Make a list of four magnetic materials.
2. Explain the difference between a magnet and a magnetic material.
3. What are the two ends of a magnet called?
4. What happens if a magnet is suspended so that it can swing freely?
5. Explain why this happens.
6. Define a "permanent magnet".
7. Define an "induced magnet".
8. Explain how magnetism can be induced.
9. What happens if:
   a) Two North Poles are brought together?
   b) Two South Poles are brought together?
   c) One North and One South Pole are brought together?
10. Describe how the field around a magnet can be plotted using a plotting compass.
11. Sketch the field around the following, using arrows to show the direction of the field:
    a) A single magnet
    b) Two magnets side by side attracting each other.
    c) Two magnets side by side repelling each other.

4.7.1.1 Poles of a Magnet and Magnetic Fields Answers

1. Iron, Cobalt, Nickel, Steel
2. A magnet has a magnetic field around it. A magnetic material can be magnetised and influenced by a magnetic field.
3. North Seeking Pole and South Seeking Pole
4. It aligns in the Earth's magnetic field with the N pointing north and the S pointing South
5. The fields of the magnetic and the Earth align exerting a force on the magnet
6. A piece of magnetic material which is always magnetised.
7. A piece of magnetic material which becomes a magnet temporarily by either …
8. …Placing the magnetic material in the magnetic field of a permanent magnet or putting the piece of magnetic material inside a solenoid with a DC current flowing through it.
9.
    a) Repulsion
    b) Repulsion
    c) Attraction
10. Place the plotting compass into the magnetic field. Record the direction in which the N Pole points. Repeat at different locations in the field.
11. Appropriate diagrams

4.7.2.1 Electromagnetism

1. Describe how the magnetic field around a wire carrying a current (as shown in the diagram below) can be demonstrated.

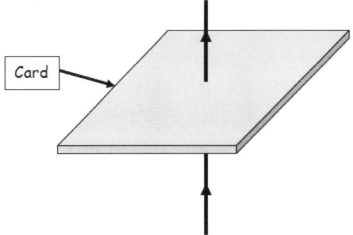

2. Describe how the pattern would change if the direction of the current was changed.
3. What is the relationship between the distance from the wire and the strength of the magnetic field?
   The strength of the magnetic field around a current carrying wire can be increased by making the wire into a solenoid.
4. What is a solenoid?
5. Describe the magnetic field pattern around a solenoid.
6. What is the relationship between the direction of the current in the solenoid and the direction of the magnetic field?
7. How can the strength of the magnetic field around a solenoid be increased?
8. Sketch and describe the operation of a magnetic door lock.
9. Sketch and describe the operation of an electromagnetic trip switch.
10. Sketch and describe the operation of an electric relay.

4.7.2.1 Electromagnetism Answers

1. Use a plotting compass to show the direction of the magnetic field at various points around the wire.
2. The field would change direction.
3. The further away, the weaker the field.
4. A coil of wire.
5. Like a bar magnet (suitable sketch)
6. Changing the direction of the current changes the direction of the magnetic field.
7. Increase number of coils, increase the current, add an iron core.
8. Suitable sketch and description
9. Suitable sketch and description
10. Suitable sketch and description

1. In what direction will the current carrying wire move in each of the following diagrams:

   a)

   b)

   c)

   d)

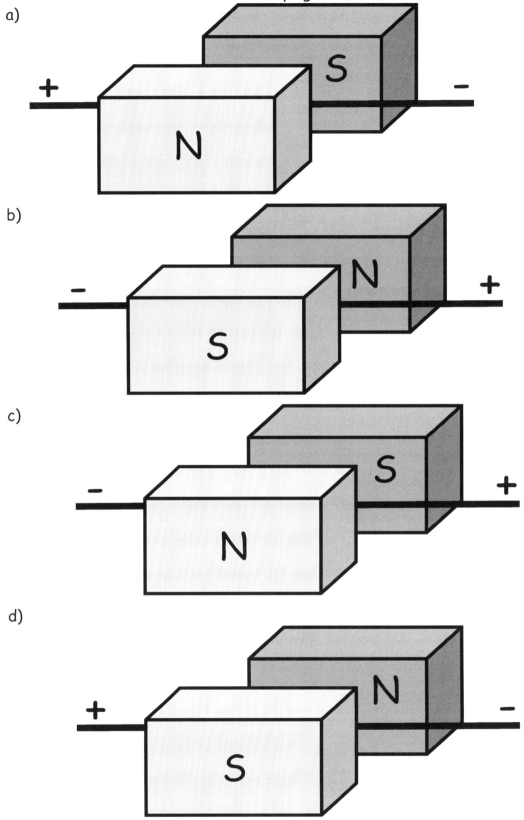

4.7.2.2 Fleming's Left-Hand Rule Answers

1a) Up
b) Up
c) Down
d) Down

Force = magnetic flux density x current x length

$$F = B I l$$

(Students should be able to apply this equation which is given on the *Physics Equation Sheet*.)

Give all answers to 2 significant figures.

1a) What is the force on a 4m long wire which carries a current of 9A in a magnetic field of 1T?

b) What is the force on a 1m long wire which carries a current of 9A in a magnetic field of 2T?

c) What is the force on a 10m long wire which carries a current of 4A in a magnetic field of 1T?

d) What is the force on a 6.4m long wire which carries a current of 4.5A in a magnetic field of 1.3T?

e) What is the force on a 1.6m long wire which carries a current of 2.6A in a magnetic field of 3.7T?

f) What is the force on a 2.9m long wire which carries a current of 1.8A in a magnetic field of 1.6T?

g) What is the force on a 510mm long wire which carries a current of 110mA in a magnetic field of 43mT?

h) What is the force on a 907mm long wire which carries a current of 3.7A in a magnetic field of 362mT?

i) What is the force on a 313cm long wire which carries a current of 708mA in a magnetic field of 85mT?

j) What is the force on a 505mm long wire which carries a current of 5.2A in a magnetic field of 768mT?

2a) Calculate the current passing through a 5m wire which experiences a force of 5N in a magnetic field of 8T

b) Calculate the current passing through a 5m wire which experiences a force of 10N in a magnetic field of 4T

c) Calculate the current passing through a 6m wire which experiences a force of 1N in a magnetic field of 9T

d) Calculate the current passing through a 5.4m wire which experiences a force of 2.7N in a magnetic field of 1.3T

e) Calculate the current passing through a 3.3m wire which experiences a force of 1.2N in a magnetic field of 5.4T

f) Calculate the current passing through a 9.9m wire which experiences a force of 9N in a magnetic field of 8.8T

g) Calculate the current passing through a 41cm wire which experiences a force of 831mN in a magnetic field of 290mT

h) Calculate the current passing through a 184cm wire which experiences a force of 0.2N in a magnetic field of 751mT

i) Calculate the current passing through a 558cm wire which experiences a force of 618mN in a magnetic field of 341mT

j) Calculate the current passing through a 829cm wire which experiences a force of 8.7N in a magnetic field of 57mT

3a) Determine the strength of the magnetic field in which a 8m long wire experiences a force of 9N when a current of 2A passes through it.

b) Determine the strength of the magnetic field in which a 4m long wire experiences a force of 8N when a current of 9A passes through it.

c) Determine the strength of the magnetic field in which a 9m long wire experiences a force of 10N when a current of 7A passes through it.

d) Determine the strength of the magnetic field in which a 8.6m long wire experiences a force of 3.3N when a current of 2.1A passes through it.

e) Determine the strength of the magnetic field in which a 6.8m long wire experiences a force of 8.8N when a current of 4.8A passes through it.

f) Determine the strength of the magnetic field in which a 7.4m long wire experiences a force of 1.4N when a current of 0.4A passes through it.

g) Determine the strength of the magnetic field in which a 793cm long wire experiences a force of 949mN when a current of 443mA passes through it.

h) Determine the strength of the magnetic field in which a 65mm long wire experiences a force of 5.6N when a current of 6.2A passes through it.

i) Determine the strength of the magnetic field in which a 512cm long wire experiences a force of 702mN when a current of 463mA passes through it.

j) Determine the strength of the magnetic field in which a 90cm long wire experiences a force of 9.4N when a current of 4.9A passes through it.

4a) A length of wire in a magnetic field of strength 1T experiences a force of 2N when a current of 1A passes through it. How long is the wire?

b) A length of wire in a magnetic field of strength 1T experiences a force of 2N when a current of 10A passes through it. How long is the wire?

c) A length of wire in a magnetic field of strength 9T experiences a force of 7N when a current of 8A passes through it. How long is the wire?

d) A length of wire in a magnetic field of strength 8.1T experiences a force of 9.4N when a current of 9.3A passes through it. How long is the wire?

e) A length of wire in a magnetic field of strength 1.2T experiences a force of 1.9N when a current of 5A passes through it. How long is the wire?

f) A length of wire in a magnetic field of strength 0.4T experiences a force of 8.1N when a current of 1.6A passes through it. How long is the wire?

g) A length of wire in a magnetic field of strength 841mT experiences a force of 140mN when a current of 4mA passes through it. How long is the wire?

h) A length of wire in a magnetic field of strength 862mT experiences a force of 0.3N when a current of 2A passes through it. How long is the wire?

i) A length of wire in a magnetic field of strength 864mT experiences a force of 507mN when a current of 601mA passes through it. How long is the wire?

j) A length of wire in a magnetic field of strength 474mT experiences a force of 8.8N when a current of 2.4A passes through it. How long is the wire?

1a) 36N
b) 18N
c) 40N
d) 37N
e) 15N
f) 8.4N
g) 0.0024N
h) 1.2N
i) 0.19N
j) 2N

2a) 0.13A
b) 0.5A
c) 0.019A
d) 0.38A
e) 0.067A
f) 0.1A
g) 7A
h) 0.14A
i) 0.32A
j) 18A

3a) 0.56T
b) 0.22T
c) 0.16T
d) 0.18T
e) 0.27T
f) 0.47T
g) 0.27T
h) 14000T
i) 0.3T
j) 2100T

4a) 2m
b) 0.2m
c) 0.097m
d) 0.12m
e) 0.32m
f) 13m
g) 42m
h) 0.17m
i) 0.98m
j) 7.7m

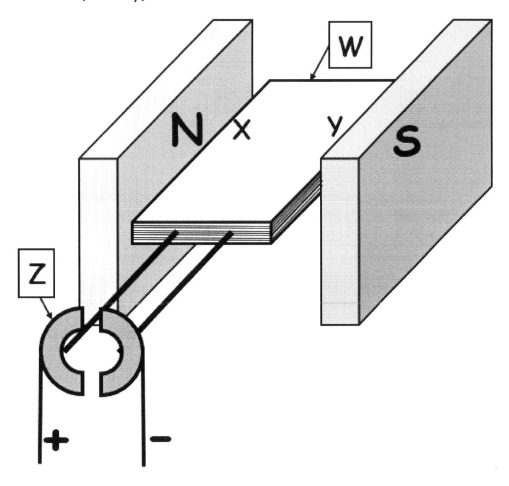

1. What is the part of the motor labelled W?
2. In which direction are the magnetic field lines?
3. In which direction is the electric current flowing at X?
4. In which direction will the coil move at X?
5. In which direction is the electric current flowing at Y?
6. In which direction will the coil move at Y?
7. Use your answers to q4 and q6 to say in which direction the coil will rotate.
8. What is the name of the part labelled Z?
9. Write a paragraph to describe how the part labelled Z ensures that the coil continues to rotate.
10. Write down 2 ways to make the coil rotate in the opposite direction. Explain how Fleming's Left Hand Rule predicts this change.
11. Write down 3 ways in which the coil can be made to rotate faster.

4.5.6.1 Electric Motors Answers

1. Coil
2. N →S
3. Front of pic to back
4. Down
5. Back of pic to front
6. Up
7. Anticlockwise (looking from front of the image)
8. Split ring commutator
9. Whichever side of the coil is connected to the positive input wire is always on the left of the image and therefore always moves down. The opposite is true for the negative side. Thus the coil always rotates in the same direction.
10. Change the magnetic field direction. Change the polarity of the wires. Must reference Flemings Left Hand Rule
11. Bigger Current, Stronger Magnet, More turns on the coil (to a point)

4.7.2.4 Loudspeakers (physics only) (HT only)

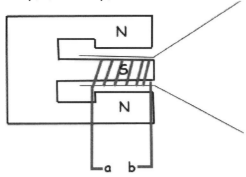

1. Label this diagram of a loudspeaker.
2. A loudspeaker converts energy between which two forms?
3. What type of current is applied between **a** and **b**?
4. Explain how the current between **a** and **b** creates movement in the cone.
5. Why does movement of the cone create sound?

4.7.2.4 Loudspeakers (physics only) (HT only) Answers

1. Magnet, coil and cone labelled correctly.
2. Electrical to Sound (vibration, kinetic)
3. Alternating
4. As the electrical potential between a and b changes, the interaction between the magnetic field due to the coil and that of the magnet changes causing the coil to move. The coil is connected to the cone so that moves.
5. The movement of the cone causes compressions and rarefactions in the air particles around it. This is a sound wave.

4.7.3.1 Induced potential and 4.7.3.3 Microphones (HT only)

1. What is needed to make an electric current?

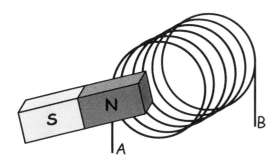

The diagram shows a magnet being inserted into a coil of wire which has 2 ends, A and B.

2. As the magnet is put into the coil, explain what happens inside the coil.
3. When the magnet is stationary inside the coil, what happens?
4. When the magnet is removed from the coil, what happens?
5. How can the induced current be increased?
6. How can the direction of the induced current be changed?
7. Give 3 uses of this effect.
8. Choose 1 of your answers to question 7. Draw a suitable diagram and explain how the effect is used.
9. A microphone converts energy from _____ to _____
10. List the main parts of a microphone.
11. Use the diagram below to describe how a microphone takes in sound energy to make electricity.

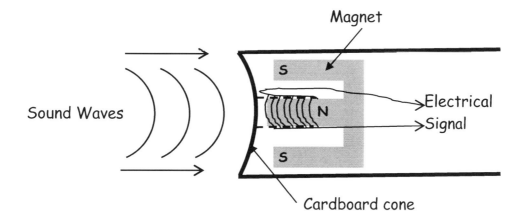

4.7.3.1 Induced potential and 4.7.3.3 Microphones Answers

1. A magnet moving in a coil of wire (or vice versa)
2. A current is induced
3. No current is induced
4. A current is induced in the opposite direction to answer 2
5. Move the magnet faster, stronger magnet, more turns on the coil
6. Change the direction of movement of the magnet
7. Generating electricity, microphone, etc
8. Appropriate diagram
9. Sound (vibration) to electrical
10. See diagram
11. Sound waves case cone to vibrate. Coil is attached to cone. Coil moves in magnetic field. Current (pd) is induced in wire. Current can be detected, amplified, etc

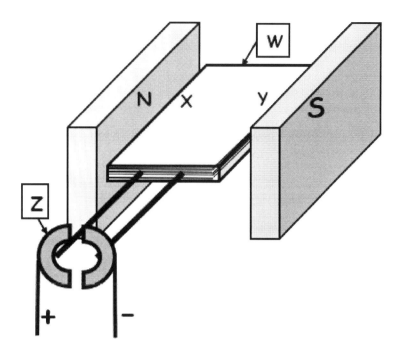

1. The above diagram shows a device for generating an electric current. Will it generate AC or DC?
2. What is the name of this device?
3. What is the name of the part labelled Z?
4. Which part is rotated?
5. List 5 methods by which this part can be rotated.
6. Explain how the rotation causes a current to be generated. In your answer, you should refer to the current in X and Y and the parts labelled W and Z along with the poles of the magnet.
7. There are no brushes on this diagram. Identify where they would be and give the role of the brushes.
8. Of what material are brushes often made? Explain the reasons for this choice of material.
9. List and explain three ways in which the current generated can be increased.
10. Sketch a graph of how the Potential Difference generated varies with time. Explain what the graph shows.

4.7.3.2 Uses of the Generator Effect 1. Answers

1. DC
2. Dynamo (DC Generator)
3. Split Ring Commutator
4. W (The coil)
5. Wind, Water, Steam, Waves, Tides, etc
6. The coil W rotates. As side X is moved upwards through the magnet, a current is induced in side X of the coil in one direction. As side Y is moved downwards through the magnet, a current is induced in side Y of the coil in the opposite direction. This causes one side of Z to become positive and the other negative. As the coil continues to rotate, side X and side Y change positions and the process is repeated.
7. Brushes connect the positive and negative wires to the split ring commutator.
8. They are made of carbon because it is self-lubricating and is a conductor.
9. i) Increase the speed of rotation – more magnetic field lines cut per second
   ii) Increase the strength of the magnetic field – more magnetic field lines cut per second
   iii) More turns on the coil – more magnetic field lines cut per second
10. The graph shows a constant P.D.

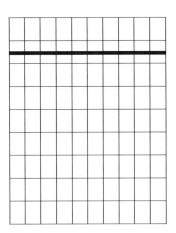

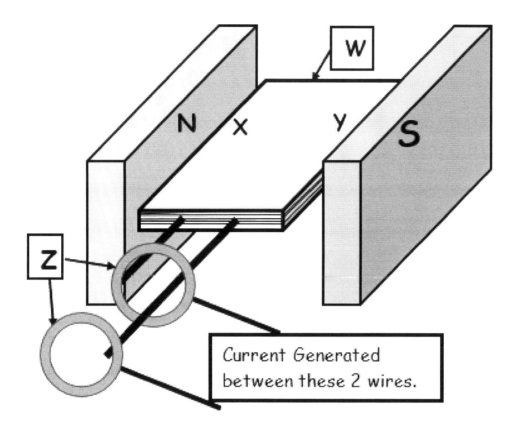

Current Generated between these 2 wires.

1. The above diagram shows a device for generating an electric current. Will it generate AC or DC?
2. What is the name of this device?
3. What are the names of the parts labelled Z?
4. Which part is rotated?
5. List 5 methods by which this part can be rotated.
6. Explain how the rotation causes a current to be generated. In your answer, you should refer to the current in X and Y and the parts labelled W and Z along with the poles of the magnet.
7. There are no brushes on this diagram. Identify where they would be and give the role of the brushes.
8. Of what material are brushes often made? Explain the reasons for this choice of material.
9. List and explain three ways in which the current generated can be increased.
10. Sketch a graph of how the Potential Difference generated varies with time. Explain what the graph shows.

1. AC
2. Alternator (AC Generator)
3. Slip Rings
4. W (the coil)
5. Wind, Water, Steam, Waves, Tides, etc
6. The coil W rotates. As side X is moved upwards through the magnet, a current is induced in side X of the coil in one direction. As side Y is moved downwards through the magnet, a current is induced in side Y of the coil in the opposite direction. This causes one slip ring to become positive and the other negative. As sides X and Y are exchanged, the polarity of each slip ring changes.
7. Brushes connect the output wires to the slip rings.
8. They are made of carbon because it is self-lubricating and is a conductor.
9. i) Increase the speed of rotation – more magnetic field lines cut per second
   ii) Increase the strength of the magnetic field – more magnetic field lines cut per second
   iii) More turns on the coil – more magnetic field lines cut per second
10. The graph shows that the potential difference varies with time from a positive value, through zero, to a negative value.

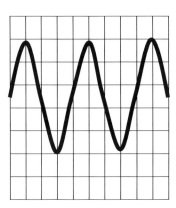

4.7.3.4 Transformers (HT only)

$$\frac{Vp}{Vs} = \frac{Np}{Ns}$$

$$V_S \times I_S = V_P \times I_P$$

(Students should be able to apply these equations which are given on the *Physics Equation Sheet.*)

Give all answers to 2 significant figures.

1a) Find the Secondary Potential Difference output from a transformer which has 400 turns on the primary coil, 10000 turns on the secondary coil and an input potential difference of 32V. Is this a Step Up or Step Down Transformer?

b) Find the Secondary Potential Difference output from a transformer which has 8000 turns on the primary coil, 6000 turns on the secondary coil and an input potential difference of 25V. Is this a Step Up or Step Down Transformer?

c) Find the Secondary Potential Difference output from a transformer which has 600 turns on the primary coil, 70000 turns on the secondary coil and an input potential difference of 89V. Is this a Step Up or Step Down Transformer?

d) Find the Secondary Potential Difference output from a transformer which has 9000 turns on the primary coil, 1000 turns on the secondary coil and an input potential difference of 98V. Is this a Step Up or Step Down Transformer?

e) Find the Secondary Potential Difference output from a transformer which has 70000 turns on the primary coil, 7000 turns on the secondary coil and an input potential difference of 30V. Is this a Step Up or Step Down Transformer?

f) Find the Secondary Potential Difference output from a transformer which has 6000 turns on the primary coil, 70000 turns on the secondary coil and an input potential difference of 139V. Is this a Step Up or Step Down Transformer?

g) Find the Secondary Potential Difference output from a transformer which has 800 turns on the primary coil, 3000 turns on the secondary coil and an input potential difference of 183V. Is this a Step Up or Step Down Transformer?

h) Find the Secondary Potential Difference output from a transformer which has 30000 turns on the primary coil, 1000 turns on the secondary coil and an input potential difference of 217V. Is this a Step Up or Step Down Transformer?

i) Find the Secondary Potential Difference output from a transformer which has 9000 turns on the primary coil, 300 turns on the secondary coil and an input potential difference of 79V. Is this a Step Up or Step Down Transformer?

j) Find the Secondary Potential Difference output from a transformer which has 700 turns on the primary coil, 5000 turns on the secondary coil and an input potential difference of 176V. Is this a Step Up or Step Down Transformer?

2a) Find the Primary Potential Difference input to a transformer which has 600 turns on the primary coil, 2000 turns on the secondary coil and an output potential difference of 166V. Is this a Step Up or Step Down Transformer?

b) Find the Primary Potential Difference input to a transformer which has 400 turns on the primary coil, 20000 turns on the secondary coil and an output potential difference of 2V. Is this a Step Up or Step Down Transformer?

205

c) Find the Primary Potential Difference input to a transformer which has 10000 turns on the primary coil, 50000 turns on the secondary coil and an output potential difference of 227V. Is this a Step Up or Step Down Transformer?

d) Find the Primary Potential Difference input to a transformer which has 4000 turns on the primary coil, 90000 turns on the secondary coil and an output potential difference of 47V. Is this a Step Up or Step Down Transformer?

e) Find the Primary Potential Difference input to a transformer which has 8000 turns on the primary coil, 800 turns on the secondary coil and an output potential difference of 14V. Is this a Step Up or Step Down Transformer?

f) Find the Primary Potential Difference input to a transformer which has 7000 turns on the primary coil, 800 turns on the secondary coil and an output potential difference of 46V. Is this a Step Up or Step Down Transformer?

g) Find the Primary Potential Difference input to a transformer which has 50000 turns on the primary coil, 1000 turns on the secondary coil and an output potential difference of 55V. Is this a Step Up or Step Down Transformer?

h) Find the Primary Potential Difference input to a transformer which has 300 turns on the primary coil, 100 turns on the secondary coil and an output potential difference of 196V. Is this a Step Up or Step Down Transformer?

i) Find the Primary Potential Difference input to a transformer which has 80000 turns on the primary coil, 50000 turns on the secondary coil and an output potential difference of 203V. Is this a Step Up or Step Down Transformer?

j) Find the Primary Potential Difference input to a transformer which has 4000 turns on the primary coil, 90000 turns on the secondary coil and an output potential difference of 217V. Is this a Step Up or Step Down Transformer?

3a) Calculate the number of turns on the primary coil of a transformer with an output potential difference of 186V, an input potential difference of 224V and 300 turns on the secondary coil. Is this a Step Up or Step Down Transformer?

b) Calculate the number of turns on the primary coil of a transformer with an output potential difference of 55V, an input potential difference of 202V and 2000 turns on the secondary coil. Is this a Step Up or Step Down Transformer?

c) Calculate the number of turns on the primary coil of a transformer with an output potential difference of 182V, an input potential difference of 155V and 500 turns on the secondary coil. Is this a Step Up or Step Down Transformer?

d) Calculate the number of turns on the primary coil of a transformer with an output potential difference of 21V, an input potential difference of 82V and 300 turns on the secondary coil. Is this a Step Up or Step Down Transformer?

e) Calculate the number of turns on the primary coil of a transformer with an output potential difference of 118V, an input potential difference of 77V and 40000 turns on the secondary coil. Is this a Step Up or Step Down Transformer?

f) Calculate the number of turns on the primary coil of a transformer with an output potential difference of 117V, an input potential difference of 182V and 20000 turns on the secondary coil. Is this a Step Up or Step Down Transformer?

g) Calculate the number of turns on the primary coil of a transformer with an output potential difference of 214V, an input potential difference of 13V and 300 turns on the secondary coil. Is this a Step Up or Step Down Transformer?

h) Calculate the number of turns on the primary coil of a transformer with an output potential difference of 230V, an input potential difference of 244V and 200 turns on the secondary coil. Is this a Step Up or Step Down Transformer?

i) Calculate the number of turns on the primary coil of a transformer with an output potential difference of 56V, an input potential difference of 212V and 90000 turns on the secondary coil. Is this a Step Up or Step Down Transformer?

j) Calculate the number of turns on the primary coil of a transformer with an output potential difference of 161V, an input potential difference of 187V and 4000 turns on the secondary coil. Is this a Step Up or Step Down Transformer?

4a) Calculate the number of turns on the secondary coil of a transformer with an output potential difference of 167V, an input potential difference of 118V and 800 turns on the primary coil. Is this a Step Up or Step Down Transformer?

b) Calculate the number of turns on the secondary coil of a transformer with an output potential difference of 154V, an input potential difference of 120V and 10000 turns on the primary coil. Is this a Step Up or Step Down Transformer?

c) Calculate the number of turns on the secondary coil of a transformer with an output potential difference of 21V, an input potential difference of 108V and 60000 turns on the primary coil. Is this a Step Up or Step Down Transformer?

d) Calculate the number of turns on the secondary coil of a transformer with an output potential difference of 34V, an input potential difference of 59V and 200 turns on the primary coil. Is this a Step Up or Step Down Transformer?

e) Calculate the number of turns on the secondary coil of a transformer with an output potential difference of 139V, an input potential difference of 207V and 700 turns on the primary coil. Is this a Step Up or Step Down Transformer?

f) Calculate the number of turns on the secondary coil of a transformer with an output potential difference of 67V, an input potential difference of 26V and 30000 turns on the primary coil. Is this a Step Up or Step Down Transformer?

g) Calculate the number of turns on the secondary coil of a transformer with an output potential difference of 37V, an input potential difference of 115V and 600 turns on the primary coil. Is this a Step Up or Step Down Transformer?

h) Calculate the number of turns on the secondary coil of a transformer with an output potential difference of 80V, an input potential difference of 109V and 8000 turns on the primary coil. Is this a Step Up or Step Down Transformer?

i) Calculate the number of turns on the secondary coil of a transformer with an output potential difference of 45V, an input potential difference of 205V and 500 turns on the primary coil. Is this a Step Up or Step Down Transformer?

j) Calculate the number of turns on the secondary coil of a transformer with an output potential difference of 207V, an input potential difference of 149V and 2000 turns on the primary coil. Is this a Step Up or Step Down Transformer?

5a) A transformer has an output potential difference of 86 V and output current of 8.4 A and an input current of 8.3A. What is the Primary Potential Difference?

b) A transformer has an output potential difference of 131 V and output current of 0.3 A and an input current of 8.7A. What is the Primary Potential Difference?

c) A transformer has an output potential difference of 12 V and output current of 6 A and an input current of 0.5A. What is the Primary Potential Difference?

d) A transformer has an output potential difference of 94 V and output current of 1.5 A and an input current of 5.6A. What is the Primary Potential Difference?

e) A transformer has an output potential difference of 65 V and output current of 4 A and an input current of 6.2A. What is the Primary Potential Difference?

f) A transformer has an output potential difference of 31 V and output current of 6.2 A and an input current of 5.8A. What is the Primary Potential Difference?

g) A transformer has an output potential difference of 96 V and output current of 9.2 A and an input current of 5.6A. What is the Primary Potential Difference?

h) A transformer has an output potential difference of 138 V and output current of 7.3 A and an input current of 1.6A. What is the Primary Potential Difference?

i) A transformer has an output potential difference of 40 V and output current of 6.2 A and an input current of 9.6A. What is the Primary Potential Difference?

j) A transformer has an output potential difference of 153 V and output current of 1 A and an input current of 3.4A. What is the Primary Potential Difference?

6a) A transformer has an input potential difference of 235 V and output current of 4.3 A and an input current of 7.9A. What is the Secondary Potential Difference?

b) A transformer has an input potential difference of 93 V and output current of 10 A and an input current of 3A. What is the Secondary Potential Difference?

c) A transformer has an input potential difference of 241 V and output current of 0.1 A and an input current of 7.7A. What is the Secondary Potential Difference?

d) A transformer has an input potential difference of 85 V and output current of 0.1 A and an input current of 4.9A. What is the Secondary Potential Difference?

e) A transformer has an input potential difference of 182 V and output current of 9.8 A and an input current of 2.5A. What is the Secondary Potential Difference?

f) A transformer has an input potential difference of 103 V and output current of 5.7 A and an input current of 3.5A. What is the Secondary Potential Difference?

g) A transformer has an input potential difference of 246 V and output current of 0.6 A and an input current of 0.5A. What is the Secondary Potential Difference?

h) A transformer has an input potential difference of 173 V and output current of 10 A and an input current of 6.4A. What is the Secondary Potential Difference?

i) A transformer has an input potential difference of 170 V and output current of 1.8 A and an input current of 1.1A. What is the Secondary Potential Difference?

j) A transformer has an input potential difference of 12 V and output current of 4.4 A and an input current of 9A. What is the Secondary Potential Difference?

7a) A transformer has an input potential difference of 20 V and output potential difference of 137 V and an input current of 5.9A. What is the Secondary Current?

b) A transformer has an input potential difference of 64 V and output potential difference of 152 V and an input current of 5.1A. What is the Secondary Current?

c) A transformer has an input potential difference of 71 V and output potential difference of 101 V and an input current of 9.3A. What is the Secondary Current?

d) A transformer has an input potential difference of 170 V and output potential difference of 3 V and an input current of 4.7A. What is the Secondary Current?

e) A transformer has an input potential difference of 99 V and output potential difference of 51 V and an input current of 9.6A. What is the Secondary Current?

f) A transformer has an input potential difference of 100 V and output potential difference of 72 V and an input current of 8.4A. What is the Secondary Current?

g) A transformer has an input potential difference of 195 V and output potential difference of 119 V and an input current of 0.7A. What is the Secondary Current?

h) A transformer has an input potential difference of 173 V and output potential difference of 39 V and an input current of 5.9A. What is the Secondary Current?

i) A transformer has an input potential difference of 128 V and output potential difference of 139 V and an input current of 5.1A. What is the Secondary Current?

j) A transformer has an input potential difference of 113 V and output potential difference of 47 V and an input current of 5.1A. What is the Secondary Current?

8a) A transformer has an input potential difference of 236 V and output potential difference of 102 V and an output current of 8.8A. What is the Primary Current?

b) A transformer has an input potential difference of 38 V and output potential difference of 157 V and an output current of 6.3A. What is the Primary Current?

c) A transformer has an input potential difference of 248 V and output potential difference of 19 V and an output current of 0.4A. What is the Primary Current?

d) A transformer has an input potential difference of 248 V and output potential difference of 17 V and an output current of 3.7A. What is the Primary Current?

e) A transformer has an input potential difference of 177 V and output potential difference of 57 V and an output current of 9.5A. What is the Primary Current?

f) A transformer has an input potential difference of 63 V and output potential difference of 207 V and an output current of 7.8A. What is the Primary Current?

g) A transformer has an input potential difference of 81 V and output potential difference of 45 V and an output current of 0.3A. What is the Primary Current?

h) A transformer has an input potential difference of 38 V and output potential difference of 249 V and an output current of 1.9A. What is the Primary Current?

i) A transformer has an input potential difference of 149 V and output potential difference of 118 V and an output current of 10A. What is the Primary Current?

j) A transformer has an input potential difference of 112 V and output potential difference of 66 V and an output current of 8.8A. What is the Primary Current?

4.7.3.4 Transformers (HT only) Answers

1a) 800 V Step Up
b) 19 V Step Down
c) 10000 V Step Up
d) 11 V Step Down
e) 3 V Step Down
f) 1600 V Step Up
g) 690 V Step Up
h) 7.2 V Step Down
i) 2.6 V Step Down
j) 1300 V Step Up

2a) 50 V Step Up
b) 0.04 V Step Up
c) 45 V Step Up
d) 2.1 V Step Up
e) 140 V Step Down
f) 400 V Step Down
g) 2800 V Step Down
h) 590 V Step Down
i) 320 V Step Down
j) 9.6 V Step Up

3a) 360 Turns Step Up
b) 7300 Turns Step Up
c) 430 Turns Step Down
d) 1200 Turns Step Up
e) 26000 Turns Step Down
f) 31000 Turns Step Up
g) 18 Turns Step Down
h) 210 Turns Step Up
i) 340000 Turns Step Up
j) 4600 Turns Step Up

4a) 1100 Turns Step Down
b) 13000 Turns Step Down
c) 12000 Turns Step Up
d) 120 Turns Step Up
e) 470 Turns Step Up
f) 77000 Turns Step Down
g) 190 Turns Step Up
h) 5900 Turns Step Up
i) 110 Turns Step Up
j) 2800 Turns Step Down

5a) 87 V
b) 4.5 V
c) 140 V
d) 25 V
e) 42 V
f) 33 V
g) 160 V
h) 630 V
i) 26 V
j) 45 V

6a) 430 V
b) 28 V
c) 19000 V
d) 4200 V
e) 46 V
f) 63 V
g) 210 V
h) 110 V
i) 100 V
j) 25 V

7a) 0.86 A
b) 2.1 A
c) 6.5 A
d) 270 A
e) 19 A
f) 12 A
g) 1.1 A
h) 26 A
i) 4.7 A
j) 12 A

8a) 3.8 A
b) 26 A
c) 0.031 A
d) 0.25 A
e) 3.1 A
f) 26 A
g) 0.17 A
h) 12 A
i) 7.9 A
j) 5.2 A

4.8 Space Physics (physics only)
4.8.1.1 and 2 Our Solar System and The Life Cycle of a Star

1. Make a list of the objects in our Solar System.
2. Our Solar System is a part of which Galaxy?
3. From what was the Sun made?
4. What force caused the particles that formed the Sun to come together?
5. Describe a white dwarf and explain how it is formed.
6. Describe a supernova and explain how it occurs.
7. Explain how a supernova is important in the production and distribution of heavy elements across the universe.
8. Describe a main sequence star and explain what is happening within it.
9. Describe a black dwarf and explain how it is formed.
10. Describe a neutron star and explain how it is formed.
11. Describe a protostar and explain how it is formed.
12. Describe a red giant and explain how it is formed.
13. Describe a black hole and explain how it is formed.
14. Describe a red super giant and explain how it is formed.
15. Make a list of the stages involved in the Life Cycle of a Star a similar size to our Sun.
16. Describe the processes involved as one stage changes into another.
17. Make a list of the stages involved in the Life Cycle of a Star much larger than our Sun.
18. Describe the processes involved as one stage changes into another.
19. Larger elements are made from smaller elements in a star. Name the process involved.
20. Explain how larger elements are made from smaller elements in a star.
21. What is the largest element that can be made in a star?
22. How are heavier elements made?
23. Most scientists agree that the Earth and our Solar System was made from at least one Supernova. Explain why they think this.

4.8 Space Physics (physics only)
4.8.1.1 and 2 Our Solar System and The Life Cycle of a Star Answers

1. Star (the sun), Planets, Moons, Asteroids, Visited by comets
2. Milky Way
3. Cloud of gas (hydrogen) and dust (Stellar Nebula)
4. Gravity
5. Small star, still emitting light formed by the collapse of a Red Giant.
6. Supernova is the explosion of a Red Supergiant. The forces inside the Red Supergiant become unable to hold it together and it explodes.
7. The largest element that can be "created" (fused) in a star is Iron. The Supernova provides sufficient energy for elements larger than Iron to be formed and the explosive force spreads them around the Universe.
8. A main sequence star is a stable one, like our sun. The main reaction inside it is 4 hydrogen atoms fusing together to make a helium atom. This causes energy to be emitted.
9. A black dwarf is formed when a white dwarf cools and stops emitting light.
10. A neutron star is a super dense star formed after a supernova. The electrons collapse into the nucleus of the atoms making up the neutron star and combine with the protons to make neutrons.
11. A Protostar is when sufficient gas has come together to form a star but it has not yet fully begun the nuclear fusion within it to be a main sequence star.
12. When a main sequence star has run out of hydrogen to fuse to helium, it begins to fuse other elements and expands to become a red giant. This only happens if the main sequence star is small (less than 5 times the size of our sun)
13. A black hole is a region of space which is so dense that even light cannot escape from it. It is formed when a red supergiant supernovas.
14. When a large (greater than five times the mass of our sun) star runs out of hydrogen to fuse, it begins to fuse other elements and expands to a Red supergiant.
15. Nebula → Protostar → Main Sequence Star → Red Giant → White Dwarf → Black Dwarf
16. Gravity draws particles of dust and gas together to form nebula. Protostar formed and when fusion begins it becomes a Main Sequence Star. When Hydrogen runs out it expands to become a red giant. Outer layers are lost and it shrinks to become a White Dwarf and then cools to a Black Dwarf.
17. Nebula → Protostar → Main Sequence Star → Red SuperGiant → Supernova then either Black Hole or Neutron Star
18. Gravity draws particles of dust and gas together to form nebula. Protostar formed and when fusion begins it becomes a Main Sequence Star. When Hydrogen runs out it expands to become a Red Supergiant. Then explodes as a supernova, forming heavy elements and throwing them across the universe. The remains collapse under gravity to form either a Black Hole or Neutron Star.
19. Fusion
20. Nuclei of small elements are drawn together by gravity eg 4 ^{1}H nuclei come together to form ^{4}He
21. Iron
22. In a Supernova due to very high energies.
23. There are elements heavier than iron in the Earth's crust.

4.8.1.3 Orbital Motion, Natural and Artificial Satellites (physics only)

1. What is meant by the term "satellite"?
2. What are the differences between a planet and a moon?
3. Give one example of a natural satellite and what it orbits.
4. Give one example of an artificial satellite and what it orbits.
5. Give 2 uses of artificial or man-made satellites.
6. The UK's satellite television services are provided by the Astra satellites. How are these satellites similar to the moon?
7. How do the Astra satellites differ from the moon?
8. Name the force which keeps both natural and man-made satellites in orbit.
9. What is the difference between speed and velocity?
10. Explain why the moon orbiting the Earth has a constant speed but a changing velocity.
11. What happens to the orbit of a satellite if its speed increases?
12. What happens to the orbit of a satellite if its speed decreases?
13. There are several reasons why engineers and scientists may need to change the orbit of a satellite. Explain briefly how this can be achieved.

4.8.1.3 Orbital Motion, Natural and Artificial Satellites Answers

1. An object (natural or artificial) which moves in orbit around another usually larger object.
2. A planet orbits a star (sun) a moon orbits a planet/dwarf planet.
3. Moon orbits the earth, etc
4. Hubble orbits the earth etc
5. GPS, Space Telescope, Spying, TV, etc
6. They orbit the earth, etc
7. They are smaller, their orbits are geosynchronous, etc
8. Gravity
9. Speed is a scalar, velocity is a vector
10. Slowing down the satellite will result in the satellite moving to a lower orbit.
11. Speeding the satellite will result in the satellite moving to a higher orbit.
12. The scientists would slow down the satellite to make it move to a lower orbit and speed up the satellite to make it move to a higher orbit.

4.8.2 Red-shift (physics only)

1. What happens to the frequency and wavelength of the sound of a car as it moves away from someone?
2. What happens to the frequency and wavelength of the sound of a car as it moves towards someone?
3. What is the name of this effect?
4. When we look at distance galaxies, what do we observe?
5. What does this show is happening to these galaxies?
6. What is the name of this effect?
7. How can scientists tell how far away the galaxy is from us?
8. If most of the galaxies we see are moving away from us, what does that tell us about the Universe?
9. How do most scientists believe the Universe began?
10. In 1998 scientists made a surprise discovery. What was that discovery and what did it tell us about the Universe?
11. There are many things that scientists do not know about the universe. What have they done and what do they continue to do to increase their knowledge?
12. What ideas have scientists proposed to explain their observations?

4.8.2 Red-shift Answers

1. The frequency decreases and the wavelength increases.
2. The frequency increases and the wavelength decreases.
3. The doppler effect
4. Light appears to be more red than it should be
5. The galaxies are moving away from us
6. Red Shift
7. The bigger the red shift, the faster the galaxy is moving and the further away from us it is.
8. The universe is expanding
9. In a Big Bang
10. Scientists observed Supernovae in distant galaxies. Distant galaxies are receding from us at an increasing rate. The universe is not slowing down its expansion – it is speeding up.
11. Continue to observe the universe and postulate new theories to explain their observations. Design new equipment (eg Hubble) to make better and more accurate observations.
12. Dark Matter, Dark Energy and Dark Flow are all ideas that need to have evidence to prove that the theories behind them are correct.

Printed in Poland
by Amazon Fulfillment
Poland Sp. z o.o., Wrocław

66100119R00129